FROM KRISHNA
TO CHRIST

FROM KRISHNA TO CHRIST

Christina Singh

authorHOUSE®

AuthorHouse™
1663 Liberty Drive
Bloomington, IN 47403
www.authorhouse.com
Phone: 1-800-839-8640

First published by AuthorHouse   05/10/2011

ISBN: 978-1-4567-6702-0 (sc)
ISBN: 978-1-4567-6703-7 (dj)
ISBN: 978-1-4567-6704-4 (ebk)

Library of Congress Control Number: 2011907125

Printed in the United States of America

Any people depicted in stock imagery provided by Thinkstock are models, and such images are being used for illustrative purposes only.
Certain stock imagery © Thinkstock.

This book is printed on acid-free paper.

Because of the dynamic nature of the Internet, any web addresses or links contained in this book may have changed since publication and may no longer be valid. The views expressed in this work are solely those of the author and do not necessarily reflect the views of the publisher, and the publisher hereby disclaims any responsibility for them.

To my beloved husband who so lovingly
Brought me to Christ and gently guided me
And shaped my life.

CHAPTER 1

The Daughter Rebels

"Papa, look, I got these carrots from Bina's house!" I shouted with glee, showing my father the big orange carrots I had plucked from my neighbor's kitchen garden. I had held my four year old brother's hand and walked across to our neighbor's compound, where I had seen the dark orange-red, very healthy looking carrots peeping out of the ground. I was fascinated and immediately wanted to reach out and pull them. Though I was only five years old, I was able to pull them out because the soil was very soft. I pulled two and took them straight to show Papa, thinking he too would be fascinated as I was.

Instead he looked at me sternly, "Who gave you these carrots?" he asked.

"I pulled them out of the ground, Papa. Nobody gave them to me," I said excitedly. "I didn't go to Bina's house. I came here to show you, how nice they look."

Whap!

I didn't know where that slap came from. My cheek stung.

"Taking things from people without permission is stealing," said Papa. "Go and return them to the neighbors and say you are sorry."

Sobbing, I went back, this time without my brother, returned the carrots and apologized. I was sad and humiliated on two counts. First, I wouldn't get to eat the luscious carrots and second, I had to go and return them to our neighbors, acknowledging that I had stolen them. I was five years old and it was an insult to my little dignity! Our neighbors kindly tried to tell me to take the carrots back, but I did not want them any more because I was so afraid of my strict father. I had learned the lesson of honesty the hard way.

I was born in a Hindu family of seven children, in Northern India, in the state of Uttar Pradesh. My family consisted of Dad and Mom, four sisters and two brothers. Papa was the one of whom I felt so scared that I never wanted to come before him, whatever the circumstances. He always seemed distant to us and was very austere and always reprimanding us. Probably the Hindu culture I was born into did not allow the father to come down to the child's level and demonstrate love in any way. I will never know why he was that way towards us. I loved Papa but was more in awe of him.

Mummy was like Papa's slave, running around waiting on him, being there at his beck and call. Sometimes I thought he was full of male chauvinism because of the way he behaved toward her. She never answered him back, never dared to retaliate. Sometimes I wondered how two people could spend their entire lives together with this kind of a strained relationship.

Is this what marriage is all about? my young brain thought.

Papa was a rich businessman, but he always kept Mummy in need of money. She was seldom able to do anything special for us girls, but when she did have money she spent it on the boys. The boys were Gaurav, the older son, and Vaibhav, my youngest and most pampered brother. They always got what they wanted. They did not even have to ask for things. They got everything on a silver platter before they even thought about it. They got beautiful new bicycles to ride. They always had pocket money to spend on whatever they liked. They were always well dressed. In contrast, we girls looked on with longing and hope. Perhaps the difference in treatment was because women didn't count in most ancient societies such as ours.

Karri, the eldest daughter, was bossy and used to boss us, the younger kids, on the sly. Arri, the second daughter, was skinny and had a belligerent attitude; Rasna and Ragna, the next two daughters, were quite insignificant. Then there was me, Vandna, who was probably the least wanted even though my name means prayer.

We were seven kids in all, five sisters and two brothers. My father was a businessman and owned two stores in a posh shopping mall of the town and had a big beautiful house set in a garden full of flowers and fruit trees. I loved playing in the garden with Vaibhav, my younger brother. My brothers seemed to be my parents' favorites, while we girls just "existed" in the house. We went to the same primary school, and Gaurav and Vaibhav were given the best of everything necessary by way of school supplies and food, while we girls were sometimes denied even the textbooks.

I needed a textbook desperately. I told Mummy.

"Mummy, I have been asking for this book for the last two weeks now. I need the book tonight; otherwise, tomorrow I will be in big trouble with my teacher."

"Call Papa on the phone and ask him to bring the book."

When I called him, he yelled at me on the phone for calling him and disturbing him at work. He never bought the book. I cried myself to sleep, and the next morning I was punished at school for not having the book.

One evening some guests were to come to our house for dinner, which was being prepared in the kitchen. The house was full of all kinds of spicy smells of dishes, but the mouth-watering smell of "kheer" (dessert made of milk, dry fruits, and rice, cooked on a slow fire) was making me hungry. The dining room was being prepared for the guests, who were to arrive at eight o'clock that summer evening.

Being only six years old at that time, I focused all my concentration on the food. I kept thinking, *when will I get to eat all those goodies*? It wasn't as though I did not get to eat nice things with the family, but since today was a special occasion and on these occasions Mummy really cooked her best, I was looking forward to nice food, especially the kheer.

I don't remember all that happened the whole day, but when evening arrived, I was put in a room with books and toys with my other brothers and sisters so that we would be out of the way not to be heard or seen. Only Mummy and Karri were allowed to serve the guests while my father ate with the guests. After the guests had eaten we children were served dinner. The boys were served first, and then the girls. I was too young to understand the discrimination and therefore none the wiser. But when the time for kheer came, which was my favorite, my younger brother was given a bowl full while I stared at him as he devoured it. My other sisters had already left the table. Probably by now they could see what was coming. I was puzzled and so asked mother, "Why don't you give me kheer to eat like you did my brother? I have been waiting for it the whole afternoon."

Without hesitation she replied with a hint of sarcasm, "Because he is a boy and you are a girl!"

I was devastated for a moment and thought, *Oh, if only I could get a taste of that kheer!*

So I hung around Vaibhav while he ate. When he finished eating and left the table, I scraped what was left in the bowl. I thought I had got the taste of my favorite dish and was somewhat gratified. But something happened in my heart and mind at that time. I fell in my own esteem and was furious with myself for longing for something that my own family, especially Mummy, never saw that I was worthy to eat, just because I was a girl. I had mixed feelings of slight satisfaction in tasting the dessert and then frustration. But I couldn't put my feelings in words. I felt ashamed of myself for scraping the bowl for leftovers and felt as though I had diminished in my own sight. For days after that, I brooded on this subject of being a girl because of which I was being deprived of all the good things in life at home, things that my brothers got in abundance.

Why was I born a girl?

I struggled with this question for a long time and then confronted my mother. "Why do my brothers get everything while we girls are deprived?"

She was surprised at my question, because in that culture girls do not question such things. However she replied to me.

"I have learned from my mother that boys are always more important than girls, and they are the ones who continue the family name. Girls go to some other family to continue somebody else's family name, so the boys need to be fed better than girls. That is why I see that your brothers are fed before I serve you girls."

We are also humans, Mummy!

In other words, she was telling me that only boys had the right for a wholesome life and existence and not girls. What a lame excuse to subjugate women and discriminate against them. *But Mummy is also a female! Why has she accepted this norm without question?*

At that young age, I found it ridiculous. Still I never forgot this episode and became very aware of not asking for any delicacy that was being cooked in our house. Be that as it may, I could not stop longing for special dishes but a change had taken place within me, and I stopped asking for anything in the future.

I rebelled.

I rebelled against the outdated traditions in a silent way. Experience had taught me that I would be naïve to think that crying or throwing temper tantrums would work. I started spending most of my time outside the house while growing up in the stifling atmosphere of discrimination.

It seemed to others that I had given in to the pressure just like my mother and my sisters had given in years ago, but I certainly had not given in. I used to control myself but burned inside with fury whenever I was in the house; but when I was playing outside, I enjoyed the company of my friends of both boys and girls in the neighborhood.

Once I got into a scuffle with a boy because he was cheating in the game of "gully danda," which we were playing. He tried to hit me after an argument, and within minutes I had him on the ground and was trying to hold him down. He tried to pull my hair so that I would let go, but he got hold of one of my earrings instead and pulled so hard that my ear was torn and started to bleed.

I had a skirt and blouse on. Vaibhav, who was standing next to me, tried to pull my skirt down, which was probably up by now and my panties showing. He probably tried to save my dignity as he couldn't save my ear from bleeding. I did not realize it; instead I thought somebody else was trying to hit me from behind. So I struck him with a backhand. I hit Vaibhav right on his face. Screaming, he ran home, and I was not able to forgive myself for hitting my little brother. Needless to say, I won the fight because I had the neighbor boy pinned to the ground until he had said sorry and promised never to cheat again. Other friends, who came from around the locality, had smirks on their faces because they were tired of his ways. He had always gotten away with cheating, but now he was paid back in full. They secretly applauded me. But I am sure if I had been beaten up by him, my girl friends would have been mad. I was very satisfied with the outcome, and that's what mattered at that time. I did get into trouble for hitting Vaibhav, even though accidentally.

My experience and events outside the house continued, while I remained subdued when I was in the house. Sometimes I climbed the "chakotra" (Indian grapefruit) trees and sat there amidst the branches for hours, thinking of ways to better my future and be capable of earning enough money to get what I wanted. This led me to study harder than my siblings. I never failed in any subject in class. My English was better than theirs because I worked very hard to improve upon it. I used to sit for hours with the English dictionary, familiarizing myself with new words, their meaning and spelling. Instead of getting overwhelmed because of discrimination, I controlled my emotions to come out victorious with flying colors. In no way was I going to give men folk of my family or society the satisfaction of sniggering at my being a female and inferior.

They loved being in a position of power because they were born male, but I would prove to them their folly by getting good grades in school and doing better in life.

There was never a day that I could recall from my childhood when I was given any kind of priority in the family, considering I was the youngest and a girl at that, whereas my younger brother Vaibhav was given kheer to eat while I looked on. As I grew up, I observed how the girls were indoctrinated to servility and how the men were put on a pedestal. I was often puzzled and often wanted to be a boy myself and sometimes cursed my fate for being born a girl. Perhaps that's what made me a tomboy. My older sisters by now were all geared to get married and live a servile life by having babies and doing chores for their families, or to put it more bluntly, to wait on the men of the family for all their worth. But I was not ready for this kind of a life. I started resenting the idea of married life.

One Sunday morning, we children were hustled into the car and Mummy said in general to all of us, "Now behave yourselves in the temple; otherwise, there will be consequences."

The Shiva temple, named after a Hindu god, was located in the center of the busy marketplace. Papa drove and Mummy sat in the front seat with Viabhav in her lap, while we six children sat on the back seat of the English made Austin that Papa was so proud of. He also had a convertible Baby Austin.

There was a lot of excitement that day because Papa and Mummy had fasted strictly for a full twenty-four hours and now were going to the temple to break their fast, to celebrate the great festival of Shivaratri, which is celebrated for the god Shiva. People whose "isht devata" (their chosen god) is Shiva fast for twenty-four hours with not even a drop of water to drink, and then they break their fast by worshiping Shiva and offering him milk and fruits. Since we were a large family, we never went to the temple together. Usually Papa went or Mummy went with Karri, but this was the first time we were going as a family.

The huge temple stood in all its glory with a giant statue of Shiva at the entrance. The walls were beautifully and artistically painted with pictures of Shiva, his wife, Parvati, and the group of his followers, which consisted of ghosts, demons and skeletons. There were hundreds of people inside the temple waiting their turn to do "pooja" (Hindu way of worship) and offer milk, fruits and money to the priest. The priest got everything because he interceded for people to the god in a strange language, supposedly Sanskrit.

Right in the middle of the temple was a huge piece of stone with a plate like structure under it. The stone was longish and seemed to be turned over on the plate. People called it "Shiva linga" and they poured milk and offered fruits and money to it. I could not understand then what that structure was but was appalled later when I came to know that the structure or "Shiva linga" was the male organ of Shiva the god. And people were worshipping it!

This was male chauvinism at its best!

I was studying in a Roman Catholic institution where many Christian girls came to study. I saw the way their fathers treated them and they told me stories of how they were loved in their families. Hearing these stories I knew our lives were absolutely opposite to theirs. *Why were we different? Was is it because they were Christians and we were Hindus?*

I always felt an emptiness, and I often wondered why I was born a girl. I could feel a weird feeling of rebellion rising in my heart and mind. I felt the need to cry out and show my feelings, but it was not worth it. Who would understand?

On the one hand, I kept working hard and getting good grades, for which I never got any appreciation at home. On the other hand, for Gaurav and Vaibhav, it was an uphill task even to scrape through their classes. Their efforts, however, were appreciated. When they started failing in class, my father hired a tutor for Gaurav, my elder brother, who had failed in all the subjects. Ironically, Vaibhav was being tutored by our eldest sister Karri.

One evening when my mother received a phone call, I saw her quite flustered. By the look on her face we knew something was wrong, but we were not told the reason. When my father came back from work, my mother was in confidential conversation with him. Suddenly my father exploded. He started yelling at the top of his voice: "Where do you think Gaurav goes? He was supposed to have gone to his tutor's house but has not been showing up at his house for almost a month, and the fee that I have already paid is wasted."

Mummy stood in silence and everybody was upset. We kids ran helter skelter to hide from my father's wrath. Apparently Gaurav had been playing hookey.

Somewhere in my mind I felt a sense of triumph and uncanny joy, that Gaurav my brother who was worshiped had not proved his worth as a boy. On the contrary I, a girl, who was belittled at every turn and twist, was doing far better at school than the demi-gods of the family. This incident gave me renewed energy and encouraged me to continue to do better and better in life. Soon Gaurav dropped from college and never completed his degree. Vaibhav also never went far in his studies, but later both brothers inherited the family business and a shop each, in the posh area of the town we lived in.

But Papa seemed to be quietly aware of the fact that I was doing pretty well in school. Once I heard him bragging to one of our relatives, "Vandna has come first in her class. She has done very well, especially in English."

I heard that and my heart swelled with pride but he never said anything to me directly. Still it felt good.

In other ways also we girls were treated differently than the boys. We were never allowed to go out without a chaperone. Going out after dark for girls was out of the question, while my older brother was always out till late night. When I was in seventh grade, I used to study at night. Mummy always asked me to open the door for Gaurav to let him in, and serve him dinner at midnight, or 1.00 a.m., or whenever he returned. I was disturbed at my studies to warm the food for him, serve it, and wait on him till he finished, and then wash his dirty dishes. This infuriated me immensely, but I had to obey Mummy, partly because we were never supposed to refuse being girls, and partly because I loved Mummy very much. In spite of everything, I knew she suffered at the hands of my father, and the tradition she was born and married into. So I did what she asked me to do.

But one night when I had warmed the food for my brother and served it, he took a long time to come to the table. I waited and waited, but after a while I decided to eat his food as I was so hungry.

I will never forget the look on his face when he came in and didn't find the meal waiting for him. He took me to task for it.

"Where is my dinner? What have you done with it?"

"Since you were taking such a long time to come, I thought you weren't hungry, so I ate it up. What's the big deal?"

He was furious. His face turned red, purple and other shades of the rainbow, because I had eaten his food, leaving him hungry and also that I had told him off. He stared at me with black eyes, sputtered a few words and went straight to Mummy with his complaint. As for me I was happy to have infuriated him. Now I did not care what happened. Thereafter he was very punctual in coming for his meal, and I was able to go back to my studies.

Getting back on my brothers in these ways was extremely gratifying, but appalling for the rest of the family because I, a girl, dared to challenge the gods of the family, quite contrary to the age old Hindu cultural establishment.

But one day my brother took his revenge. I had recently had my eyebrows plucked and shaped and felt very proud of it since it gave me a new sense of confidence in my looks, but when Gaurav saw me he mockingly asked, "What have you done to your eyebrows? You look so stupid, like a Cheshire cat!"

"For your kind information it is known as "threading," I said, choking back a sudden wave of anger.

"Whatever it is called, stop it. Don't let me see you doing it again."

I seethed. Though I did not answer him back, I did not stop.

As I grew up I tried to talk to Mummy about discrimination against girls and women. Her usual answer was, "Beti (daughter) it is right to follow age old traditions, because we have to live in this society."

But sometimes she talked about how her in-laws had treated her and how they had instigated Papa to beat her up. This infuriated me so much that I burst out, "Why do you endure all this abuse? Why don't you leave Papa and go somewhere else?"

"I cannot leave your Papa in spite of the ill treatment; I have no other place to go to, besides I have to think of all of you."

This saddened my heart, and made my hatred for marriage even stronger. And thus I resolved never to get married but become a nun instead, because I knew nuns did not marry. I really liked the way Sister Joanna, my school principal, carried herself. She looked so dignified and pure in her white habit. She was slim and tall and always walked straight. I just could not trust a Hindu man as my husband, and began dreaming of entering a Roman Catholic monastery, always having Sister Joanna in mind, as my role model.

There was an infirmary in my school, beyond which was the living quarters of the nuns. Just to get a peek at their style of living I would fake illness so that I would get to go to the infirmary. I would wait for the nurse to go, and then I would quietly sneak up, open the door a little, to peep into the nun's rooms to see what I could see. They had such a beautiful dining hall with big brass flower pots, with flowers, in every corner. It was spotlessly clean and shining. I felt I belonged there. Each time I encountered a nun in school, I was enthralled. They were different somehow. They were gentle and loving and cared for the girls. It was so very different from my home environment.

Since the time I started having some understanding of life, I resented what I saw around me at home. I resented the treatment that was meted out to Mummy by Papa. For years, when I was growing up, I had seen Mummy pleading with my father for money, so that she could feed us and get us our school supplies etc., but he never gave her enough.

The reason for not giving Mummy enough money was not poverty. Papa had a flourishing business of electrical goods, two shops, and a huge farm. Therefore he was a rich man, but it was to oppress Mummy and us so much that we could never have strength to fight back. We were always kept in need of things; the purpose seemed to be to crush our spirits so that Papa could emerge as the god, to whom we all must look up to.

My elder sister's marriage was arranged and she was married off when I was in high school. She too was treated by her husband in the traditional way. I remember one incident very clearly, which took place in Karri's house when I was visiting her.

One evening we were sitting and talking on the porch, and since I was just a teenager, I was distracted and did not pay attention to the adult's conversation. Suddenly I heard my brother-in-law tell my sister, "If you even think of doing that, I will turn you out of the house and you will be on the streets!" Hearing his tone I was jolted back to paying attention to the conversation, and immediately I jumped up and said to him, "How dare you talk to my sister like that? Do you think she is alone in the world? You have married her, so you cannot throw her out of the house. Don't you threaten her like that again."

There was silence for a while. Then my brother-in-law glared at me menacingly, got up and walked inside. My sister was furious with me for disrespecting her husband and was scared that he would take it out on her. Sure enough, when she went inside the house later, there was a scene. My father was called, the whole incident was related to him and I was sent back home. Back home I was given a lesson of my life—that in the Hindu culture the husbands are always right and women can never dare to be disrespectful to the men, no matter what! I realized that when I grew up and if I got married, my husband would have to be my god. I was confused when I was growing up and very upset when I saw the women of my family slaving after their husbands as gods. I wasn't going to take any of that crap.

My desire of becoming a nun was reinforced.

CHAPTER 2

Meeting Jesus For The First Time

The British had ruled over India for more than two centuries. Therefore we had several educational institutions they had established for their children, which were run by the State, as the Monarch of England is the synonymous Head of the State and Church. There are other institutions and schools run by various religious denominations. It was a matter of status for Indians (for Rajahs, Maharajahs and Chiefs) to send their children to Christian schools, as they could qualify for higher education in England. Thus the elite Indians, like Gandhi, Nehru, Patel and Jinnah etc. went to such schools and finished their education in England. It was Lord Macaulay's policy known as "The Filtration Theory," which was educating the classes which would filter down to the masses. Those Indians who could afford it, sent their kids to these schools as they were very expensive.

However the non-Christian Indians were strictly opposed to conversion of their children to Christianity. They still are, though they did not mind the Anglicized education they paid for.

So, our rich Papa, sent us seven kids to St. Mary's Convent School, owned by Roman Catholics. I am sure if my father had known that one of his offsprings would one day convert to Christianity, despite the opposition and persecution, he would never have sent me there. But boy, am I glad he did!

When I was a student of second grade, St. Mary's Convent School had other, even greater effects and influence on me. It was run by nuns from England and Germany. The nuns were mainly in administrative and teaching positions, and Sister Joanna was the Principal. She was very strict but genuinely cared for the children. She hated latecomers and had a nice way of using her umbrella to give them a nudge sometimes. We were all apprehensive of her umbrella. The other nuns were equally loving and caring towards the children, but I was in awe of them because they all looked alike to me in their white habits and kind faces. Sister Joanna stood out because she was slim and tall, and always carried her dreaded umbrella.

One morning Sister Joanna entered our class room, and instantly there was absolute silence. We sat silently looking at the intimidating personality of our tall and beautiful Principal, in a white habit, with some papers in her hand. She talked to our teacher for a while and then addressed us, "Children, here are some pamphlets for you to take home. Show them to your parents and if they allow you, show them to your friends and relatives." Having said that she began giving us a rectangular piece of paper, with a picture of a man in the middle, whose face was full of compassion and his hands were outstretched, attempting to catch a child falling from a height of some kind. The name JESUS was written across the top of the pamphlet, and as I recall, something else was written, but I do not remember what it was. I held the picture of that man in my hand, and was quite taken up for a moment as the child, a girl, was about my age. The black pencil sketch on white paper seemed to come alive and became deeply impressed in my memory, especially the penetrating eyes of Jesus which were exceedingly compassionate and full of love. Though I did not know exactly who Jesus was, but I could identify myself with that girl and could see that the Man Jesus was ready to save her from falling to her death. The picture was worth more than a thousand words. It seemed to be speaking to me, and I could feel a strange sense of safety in those hands. It was a feeling I have never been able to put in words. Those penetrating eyes have always been an enigma for me. Since that moment I have not been able to forget the name and face of the man called Jesus. It made such an impact on my young mind that even today I can recall every detail.

I kept looking at the picture, staring mystified, enchanted and reading His name over and over and then lowering my voice I asked my fellow student named Nalini, "Who is this Jesus?"

Nalini was a Christian so she simply said, 'This is Jesus Christ."

I remained quiet and thinking for a long time, and then asked her again, "Who is Jesus Christ?"

"I don't know, ask Miss Hoggs," she replied.

13

Miss Hoggs was our class teacher who was an Anglo—Indian. She was short, stout and motherly, so I asked her, "Miss Hoggs, who is Jesus Christ?"

She tried to explain to me who Jesus was but I found it very complicated at that time, so she promised to bring me a book to read.

The next day Miss Hoggs, brought me a book called Bible Stories for Children. I saw pictures in the Bible, and I realized that Miss Hoggs wore similar kind of dresses.

In this Bible I met Jesus for the first time. The first story I read was the birth of Jesus. I came to know who Jesus and His parents were and marveled at the little baby Jesus, not forgetting the grown up Jesus I had seen in that picture. There were other parables that Jesus told, for example "The Good Samaritan" and "The Lost Coin," and I remember thinking how foolish it would be to go on looking for the lost coin and then rejoice when you found it. I did not understand the significance of the parable at that time.

I also remember the story of Prodigal Son very well, because I remember my imagination did overtime, especially when the prodigal son had to eat what pigs ate. But my all time favorite was the story of Christmas because I got to see baby Jesus. The book was like a magnet beckoning me to read the stories over and over again, before I returned it to the teacher.

After reading the Bible Stories, my hunger for such books and stories became insatiable. I constantly pestered my teacher for more books and went out of my way to make Christian friends, so that I could borrow books from them, which I did. I read everything about Jesus I could get hold of in my school years, and there I came to know that Jesus was the Son of God and Mary was His Mother. I was too young to go further than names so I hung on to the name "Mary." Very soon I became obsessed with this name and wanted to change my own name Vandna, to Mary, because in my mind this name would identify me to Jesus.

I felt that the name Mary, was the only way to get closer to Jesus, because I was too young to know any better. I did not even understand why I wanted to be near Jesus; the feeling became an obsession. I went about my house telling my family about Jesus Christ, but was sometimes ignored as being "just a child." Sometimes I ended up irritating everyone, because they knew who Jesus was, and were not pleased to see me so enamored with the name and Person of Jesus.

One person I never spoke about Jesus to, was Papa. The whole family was so scared of Papa, but sometimes his actions took me by surprise. 1 was once very ill with typhoid and my father who never visited us on our sick-bed, or as a matter of fact never came near us, came and sat next to me and asked how I was. "Are you hungry?" he suddenly asked.

Not able to comprehend his reason for coming to see me, and scared beyond measure, I said, "Yes, I'm hungry," in a hesitant tone, turning my head away and staring out the window.

He called out to Karri, and asked her to bring something for me to eat. She brought a plate of plain boiled rice, with hot, spicy meat curry, poured over it. As I sat on the bed trying to eat, with mixed feelings of fear and wonder at Papa's behavior, I went through various emotions and felt a longing of this incident to take place more often in my life. I wished Papa would show this love for me and my sisters more, even though it was done rather sternly.

I was overwhelmed with joy and disbelief, because 1 had just seen a glimpse of love in Papa's action, of coming down from his high horse and sitting down with his sick child. I wondered what kind of a father Jesus would make. *If only Jesus was my Papa, I wouldn't be scared at all!*

My eighth birthday was drawing near. I was much excited about it, and was looking forward to it. I knew Mummy would sew a dress for me.

I asked her, "Mummy, what are you going to give me on my birthday?" She said, "But you still have five months to go; what is the hurry?" I heard Papa in his deep voice asking, "When is your birthday?" I was surprised that he had heard our conversation. I had not seen him entering the room, and was scared to answer his question.

Mummy said, "It's in August." As far as I know that was the end of the conversation. I shot out of the room as soon as I got the opportunity, far away from Papa's presence.

After two or three days had passed, my mother brought me a packet and asked me to open it. When I opened the packet, I was dumbfounded. It contained the most beautiful dress I had ever seen. It was pink with a lot of frills and laces, and what have you.

"Papa has brought this for your birthday," she said. I was overjoyed and wondered at the change in Papa's attitude towards me. However Papa wouldn't give the gift directly to me. I ran around the house showing it to everyone. For five months I hugged the dress to myself and waited for the day I would be allowed to wear it. Mummy had kept it safely in her suitcase. I was not allowed to wear it before my birthday. I got to wear it to school on the day my birthday was celebrated, by taking a lot of treats for all of my friends.

This was the best birthday I could remember, and the only birthday gift from Papa. But the fact that my father had bought a birthday gift for me made me all the happier, though I never received a gift from him ever again thereafter.

My family was devout Hindu, and worshipped several gods and goddesses. The main ones being Krishna, Ram, Sita, Brahma, Vishnu and Shiva. My parents were very regular in performing "pooja," which is done with all fanfare and chanting of "mantras," and burning of incense etc. The family enjoyed these rituals and participated in them with great fervor. Somehow, I was quite bored with such meaningless pooja before idols of clay, and only enjoyed the part where we got to eat the "prashad." Prashad is sweets, after being offered to gods, perhaps like Holy Communion. I continued to enjoy eating prashad, until I was grown up enough to understand the futility of worshiping idols. I say futility because the situation of the females in the house never seemed to improve. We were always the lesser beings, which infuriated me no end.

Did Vishnu or Shiva mistreat their wives that way? I mused.

The complexity of religion is mostly lost to the people who practice it. I have often heard people trying to make religion seem very simple by saying, "All religions have one message as they all point to one God. They have different names but all religions teach practically the same thing." But that is not the case.

In India, ancient Hinduism is the mainline religion with more than thirty-three million gods and goddesses, whereas in Christianity there is only one God. Furthermore, in Hinduism they make statues of gods and goddesses, before which they bow down and worship those images. In Christianity according to the second Commandment, making of images of any kind and worshiping them, is strictly forbidden. When I participated in worship with my family, I did not think much about it and joined in, because I was a child and imitated whatever everybody else did. I did look at the idols and plenty of feelings of fear, and sometimes wonder, mixed with revulsion, swept through me, which gave rise to confusion. I could not figure out why living, intelligent human beings, worshiped animals and inanimate objects.

The observance of *caste system* is another factor that has been a draw back to the society of India. It has severe restrictions for the "lower" caste people, who are known as "untouchables" or the outcasts of society—all due to their bad "karma" (deeds) in their previous life.

Furthermore women are treated like *possessions*. Their duty is to bear sons (not daughters) for their husbands (imagine a generation of only boys). If the wife, by any chance bears only daughters, her life is made miserable by the in-laws and the husband. The popular belief is that to be born a woman was, because of some sin in their former life. So the girls were killed immediately after their birth or thrown in garbage cans, for scavengers to eat. Another reason to kill the girls is the tradition of dowry. Parents tend to get rid of their daughters because they know they will have to give dowry to their daughters, husbands and in-laws, while the sons bring in dowry! But it doesn't end there. The girls who are married are also in danger of being killed, generally by fake accidental burning while cooking, which is also called "bride burning." And this practice of burning brides for dowry is still quite common. In many cases even the authorities look away and register accidental death. And the husband is free to marry again, collect another dowry and burn again. So much for paganism.

Through the centuries people have self-interpreted traditions and turned them around to suit themselves, for their own good. For example the tradition of *dowry* was initially established to help the newly married couple, to start their own home. The bride's parents gave her jewels and most of the household goods, which are necessary when you make a new home. Parents gave gold and jewels so that their daughters and family would have something to fall back upon, should something happen to her husband, and she was left alone in the world. But this has been distorted by the so called patriarchs of the society, and today the young brides are burnt alive for the lust of money.

In India when a marriage takes place, it is seldom between couples. The marriage is more or less between families, which means that the families arrange marriages and collectively make the decisions for the couple being married. Especially the issue of how much dowry to demand from the bride's parents is discussed at length and a lot of bargaining goes on between the two sides. Much depends on the qualifications of the groom, whether a doctor, lawyer or engineer or a petty clerk.

Sometimes the bride's parents consent to give a certain amount of money as dowry, but are unable to keep their promise. Or sometimes the groom and his parents get greedy after receiving the money and want more. On either occasion the bride's life is at stake. To get more dowries, the groom and his parents need to get rid of the bride to leave the door open for a second marriage, and a second round of dowry. What is better than sprinkling some kerosene oil on the bride, putting a match to her, and later telling everyone including the police that she had committed suicide, or had burnt herself accidentally while cooking? Doesn't that sound easy? For some people who lust after money and are greed personified, it *is* easy. I had witnessed many such inhuman traditions in my former religion, which naturally turned me off. There is no dignity for women, nor any value for human life. Somewhere I'd read that Jesus said, "You cannot serve God and mammon at the same time." Incidentally, the Hindu goddess of wealth is Laxmi, the wife of Vishnu.

I had read many Bible stories, and somehow I found them so meaningful, attractive and humane that I started questioning the Hindu religious rituals and practices. I started having doubts and questions in my mind, which I could neither figure out on my own, nor put in words. So I began questioning the Hindu faith, but I never had the courage to speak out against it. I could not go against my mother, because I loved her very much. But it seems the Bible stories helped me to form doubts in my mind about Krishna and Shiva, whom my mother worshiped, and yet they never got her out of the predicament that she was in. She was the person who cooked and cleaned and waited on all the men folk of the house, including her own sons, and was treated like a slave by them all. She had no vacation, or free time for herself. No men folk came to help her. How long would she and other orthodox Hindu women have to endure this loathsome tradition?

Since the moment I met Jesus for the first time, I have striven to know more and more about Him who has moved me so much. He was so thoughtful towards all women. Jesus gave due respect to His mother. His first missionary preachers were women—the Samaritan woman at the well, and Mary at the empty tomb on that first Easter morning.

There was a chapel in my school and I felt drawn towards it, even though I was a Hindu and therefore forbidden to enter therein. During break time we three younger sisters generally stayed together, the older two had their own group.

It was exceedingly difficult for me to slip into the chapel as my sisters were always around, but one day I did not join them for lunch, instead made my way and slipped inside the chapel quietly. What an awe inspiring atmosphere! I felt the sound of silence was amazing. What serenity and how peaceful it was! Even at that young age I was spellbound, looking at the altar and the crucifix; not knowing what it was all about, being very different from the Hindu temples that we were taken to.

In that chapel I was hypnotized. That calmness in my heart and mind, which somehow eluded me in the Hindu temples, even in that young age, uplifted me. Maybe that is why that feeling of wonder and the atmosphere in the chapel are still embedded in my mind. I felt glued to the place and wanted to stay.

I was oblivious to the world when I heard the school bell and realized I was in big trouble because I had missed lunch and my sisters would be looking for me.

Sure enough my sister questioned me, "Where have you been? You have not had your lunch."

We were in the same class and she had been asked to keep an eye on me. She had probably seen me coming out of the chapel or guessed it. I just shrugged my shoulders and looked at her angry face. She turned and walked off. At home she told Mummy, and I was severely reprimanded and was warned never to go to the chapel again or . . .

Nonetheless, I was drawn to that chapel by some inner mysterious force, so I went to the chapel, whenever my sisters were not watching, or when I could give them the slip. Lunch was a big affair with packed lunch boxes, brought especially with hot food right at lunch time by a servant of the house. We were supposed to eat every bit of that lunch, and the empty lunch boxes inspected later by Mummy. Therefore it was not advisable to skip lunch, and also I did not want my stomach to growl during class.

In my quiet way, I went on pursuing my quest for the knowledge of Christ. I made friends with Christian girls in my class, and started visiting them in their homes. All my growing years I was constantly the butt of my siblings' jokes, and a subject of ridicule because they said I was different. My adolescent years were spent in confusion and fear, because I was a girl, and so had no freedom of speech, movement or thought whatsoever. But it was my insistence on knowing more about Jesus and Christianity, which became a constant irritant for all around me. My family was angry with me for trying to identify myself with Christians, and mocked me openly, before the guests and friends who came over.

However I had my own agenda and determined to follow it regardless of consequences. This constant tussle between my family and me, turned me into a recluse. I kept to myself and read everything I could get hold of, about Jesus and His teachings. Perhaps contra-suggestion was doing overtime. My behavior bothered my folks. They thought I was conceited or defiant because I no longer argued with them. I became like an introvert and kept to myself to avoid unpleasantness.

My favorite spot was the garden, and favorite past time was climbing trees. There were times when in the afternoons, I would climb trees and plucked half ripe fruit from the trees and brought them quietly inside, when Mummy was taking a nap. I would sprinkle a lot of red hot pepper powder and black salt on it, and enjoyed eating the fruit. Before Mummy woke up I cleaned up, so she wouldn't know what I had been up to. Actually she thought I too was taking a nap as the others. It was fun. Sometimes Vaibhav and I quietly crept out with bicycles, while Mummy took her nap. One day it was raining and Vaibhav was not in the mood to go out, so I went by myself. I took two rounds safely on the big bicycle which belonged to Gaurav, but on the third round the bicycle slipped, and I landed on the ground, hurting my leg. There was a big gash on the left calf, which bled profusely. Seeing the blood I got scared. Limping inside I showed the wound to Karri, who quickly bandaged it, but Mummy and others could easily see the bandage.

The bicycle was confiscated.

When I was about eighteen years old, I received a brass cross with a chain as a gift from a Christian friend of mine. It had the figure of Jesus on it. That cross became my prized possession and I cherished the gift. I held that necklace with the cross in my hand, and felt a great longing to wear it, to identify myself with Jesus. Scared of my people, I did not wear it at home until one morning I found the courage to wear it to college.

When I returned home, my mother demanded, "Where did you get the cross from?" So I told her that one of my friends had given it to me.

She gave me a severe telling off and threatened to tell my father. But somehow I felt the threat was hollow. My father was never told anything regarding the children, because Mummy knew the results would be devastating. So she told Karri, Arri and Gaurav about my inclination towards Christianity, but never mentioned it to Papa, as I knew she wouldn't.

Nevertheless, I could see the repercussions of this conversation on Mummy and my siblings. The environment became tense and one of secrecy. They stopped talking whenever I appeared.

Was I a threat to them? Were they scared of society or of my leaving them, and making them a laughing stock in their circles?

It was evident that I was branded a radical, and they were afraid I was ready to step out contrary to Hindu faith. I was not pleased with the idea of being beaten, or locked up in a room or marrying me off to some Hindu before I took that step. The last measure would really seal my fate and doom.

However, one evening Mummy came to me and said, "Why do you go on about Christianity like you do? Why don't you realize that you are born in the Hindu faith and you will have to remain loyal to the religion of your birth? If the gods wanted you to be a Christian they would have caused you to be born in a Christian home."

Gaurav had followed her into my room with a mocking expression on his face, which infuriated me.

"I know that I am born in the Hindu faith, but I can't help being drawn to Jesus Christ who loves us, and is always there with open arms, to save us from hurting ourselves like in that picture I saw. No Hindu god loves or helps us when we are in trouble. We must do it by our own karma. I just like Him so I talk about Him, so what?" I replied wearily.

Mummy replied scornfully, "You are no longer a child, and let me warn you that if your father hears of this he will do something drastic, and you will have to regret it all your life. It is in your best interest that you shake yourself out of this rebellion."

She left my room with Gaurav following. Mummy had never spoken to me sternly like that before. I knew immediately that she was deeply distressed, but Jesus gently continued to call me. What was I to do? On the one hand was my mother, whom I loved deeply, on the other I felt strongly drawn to Christ.

Would Mummy ever understand my torn feelings?

No, I suppose not. But what could I do to make her, or anyone else understand? How could I continue my quest without hurting Mummy's feelings? I did not want to hurt her, as she had enough troubles of her own.

CHAPTER 3

My Mother And I

A petite girl with rosy complexion, black long flowing hair that reached below her waist, an innocent face, big black eyes and pink lips, aged about fourteen years, altogether beautiful, sits in an ancient Indian kitchen where logs are burning in the stove, and a pot full of lentils is cooking merrily. The girl, whose name is Veera, is sitting in the kitchen for company to her mother, and talking to her casually, while the mother tries to fix dinner for her large family. Veera is sitting close to the fire which is making her face rosier due to the heat from the fire.

She is her father's favorite daughter. She was the first born, and the most beautiful of all his children. Just when Veera sat in the kitchen with her face flushed, her father walked in, saw her and said to his wife, "Why can't you keep Veera out of the kitchen and do the work by yourself? Don't you know the heat from the fire makes her face flushed, and might ruin her complexion? Someday I am going to marry her off to her prince charming. "

Veera's mother looked at her husband with narrowing furious eyes, thinking—*He should be spoiling the boys not Veera, since she will be going to somebody else's house soon—prince charming ha!*

But she said nothing. Her husband held Veera's hand and took her to another room, away from the kitchen. The mother did not understand why her husband made much of Veera's beauty. This behavior of his made her angry. Her mother always said girls were never to be spoiled, because no one knew what kind of family they would be married into.

The Hindu culture does not allow women to back chat to their husbands because the husband was supposed to be her god, so she sat silently, grinding her teeth in frustration, and made a resolution—

I am going to train my daughter to cook whether he likes it or not. Without knowing the art of cooking, I would find it difficult to find Veera the right husband. What would her future in-laws say if Veera does not learn how to cook? They would turn her out of the house, and that would be detrimental.

Making this resolution for the good of her daughter, made her happy and she continued with her work.

Veera had a beautiful voice and soon became a radio artist, singing solos and leading groups as she grew up. She also sang "bhajans" (religious songs) at the funeral of Mahatma Gandhi, who is regarded as the father of the Indian nation.

Veera was my mother, who was the first born in the family of five. She was thoroughly pampered by her father. But her mother knew what lay in her daughter's future, so she had Veera's feet firmly planted on the ground. She never let her think that life would be easy for her as a wife. She never let Veera's beauty go to her head, although in her heart of hearts Veera knew that her beauty was exceptional. But being pretty did not bring happiness in Mummy's life. She got married to Papa, who was by no means a prince, when she was only seventeen years of age. I'm sure she must have had dreams of marrying a handsome and loving husband. I often wondered how their first few years of married life were spent; whether they were happy, or did the in-laws interfere in their lives as they are wont to do in India.

I had heard that Papa was quite good looking in his youth. Age had little effect on him. He was still good looking at the age of sixty. He had fine white and even teeth, often exposed when he smiled, which he reserved for outsiders. He too had black eyes, and black wavy hair like mother. He always dressed meticulously and drove an expensive car, made in England. He was, and looked wealthy, and acted as though he owned the world. So Mummy did marry a good looking man, but did he love her at all? I will never know. Though he made her pregnant and made her bear him children, five in a row, in quick succession, which kept her extremely busy cooking, cleaning and caring for new arrivals at short intervals. I didn't think it was a gentlemanly act.

There is a custom in India, of the woman of the house covering her head in the presence of her in-laws with a part of the "sari," and touching their feet, out of respect. Mummy always observed this rule. She was slavishly obedient to Papa's commands, and demands, and was a hard working hostess at his parties and dinners. She had no say in arranging the marriage of any of her daughters. It was always Papa who arranged the marriage with the help of his uncle and aunt and the priests. Nobody else had any say in the matter, because that was the custom and culture we were born into.

Soon Papa arranged the marriage of the two older daughters. Karri was married off to a man from the military, who after retirement started his own business, and Arri was married to someone who was a CEO in a factory. Mummy worked extremely hard in those lavish weddings. She supervised all the catering. It is extremely tough to see that all in-laws (of extended family), are served with much care. One slip and she would be taunted for it for the rest of her days. She would slog for days before the marriage, and be on her toes, until each relative left after the marriages were over. Hindu weddings take at least three days, because there are several rituals and customs that have to be completed before the bride can leave for her husband's house.

Soon after marriages of both our sisters, we started hearing news of Karri being ill-treated and beaten by her husband, which unnerved Mummy and she started worrying about the future of the rest of her daughters. She often shared Karri's woes with me.

One day I asked her why Karri endured such ill-treatment from her husband. "Why doesn't she come back home and live with us again?"

Almost chokingly she answered, "She thinks about the future of you girls. If she leaves her husband and comes back home, it would reflect on the family adversely. It would tarnish the reputation of your sisters, and you, and no decent family would like to marry you in to their family. That's how things are in our Hindu culture."

This certainly did not make sense to me. How could Karri's coming back home affect our marriage? That meant she would have to endure the ill treatment of her husband and stick with him forever. The custom probably came into being to avoid divorce, but evidently has been distorted by wicked men, like the practice of dowry.

After the first year of their marriage, Karri had a son whom they named Manoj. Mummy promptly sent a lot of stuff to Karri's in-laws, hoping they would treat her more kindly, since she had given them an heir. Things did soften a little and Mummy became a little happier that Karri was busy with her son. Karri also brought Manoj to visit us, and we instantly took a liking to him, especially Mummy. She was absolutely taken up with her grandson and crooned and played with him for hours. Years rolled by and Mummy's relationship with her first grandson deepened. He became very special to her.

One evening Papa came back early from his shop and said, "Manoj is missing from school; no one knows where he is; he has not returned home." Mummy stared blankly ahead of her, and started crying softly. We were all so shocked that no one could say anything.

It seems Manoj was in school when a person came and said that his family wanted him home early because his father had suddenly taken ill. The teacher let him go, but this was not true. He was kidnapped by the thug who quickly picked him up and disappeared. The man later called and demanded a ransom of 50,000 rupees (equivalent to about $1,000.00) by calling Karri's husband and in-laws. They were rich people so could afford to pay up. This news shattered everyone especially Mummy. It felt as though someone had died in the house, and for days there was no proper food cooked, and Mummy just sat and prayed. All of us seemed to be suddenly overcome with grief. There was silence in the house and everyone just waited breathlessly for the phone to ring again, to get to know the next step from the abductor.

A whole week dragged by, and then we heard that Manoj was found lying drugged and unconscious with soiled clothes, in a small barn near a stream. The story we heard was that the man who kidnapped Manoj, was their neighbor's son, who wanted to buy a jeep. Knowing that Manoj's grandparents were wealthy business people, he decided to kidnap him and ask for ransom. Manoj went with him without hesitation because the guy was well known to the family, and Manoj addressed him as "Uncle." The kidnapper who was reputed to be a bad lot, kept him holed up in the barn quite far from the city. He fed him little food, and kept him drugged to keep him semi-conscious.

One early morning someone who was a friend of Manoj's grandfather, and the kidnapper's father, was driving by the outhouse and saw the kidnapper near it. He wondered why this guy was hanging around the outhouse. Since he had heard about the kidnapping he became suspicious and called the police. The police arrested the kidnapper and rescued Manoj.

There was great joy all around, especially for Mummy. But this had affected her much. She became more religious and spent more time in singing religious songs and praying. She wanted us to sing with her while she played the "harmonium" (an Indian instrument). Just to please her, I sometimes sang along with her. But those religious songs about Hindu dieties never gave me peace and solace, as the thought of Jesus did. Later mother also started talking more about the ill treatment that was meted out by Papa to her. Previously she used to dismiss my questions about being ill-treated by Papa.

Incidentally, it was interesting to know that Arri was not abused by her husband or in-laws. On the contrary her husband was "henpecked" and therefore Arri ruled the roost. But it did not come out in the open until her mother-in-law died. Arri's father-in-law had passed away before her marriage. We saw Arri calling the tune in the house, making decisions disregarding her husband. This was something that none of us could understand, since husbands were supposed to be superior to wives, and head of the family, but I liked the reversed order of Hindu culture in that house!

Why not? Why can't women be superior to men sometimes? If only they'd use their heads.

And that reminds me of a man who was boasting in public, about being the head of the family. The man was saying, how as head of the house, whatever he said, was carried out without any objection, discussion or delay. His wife was standing next to him, listening patiently to his raving and ranting about himself being the absolute head of the family, and what have you! When she'd heard enough, she gently interrupted him, and said in a matter of fact manner—"By the way, who turns that head?"

Now I was in college and had begun to understand most of the mindless subjugation of women that went on in my house. Also I had started talking to my mother more than before. I knew Mummy was experiencing a change in herself. I wondered what was triggering this change. She had also started resenting the ill treatment from her husband, and her in-laws. I knew somehow that she was a bitter person inside, but never could share her feelings with us for fear of social pressure.

Rasna and Ragna were too preoccupied, dreaming about their own future husbands, to notice any change in Mummy, but I did. I felt closer now to her in her grief and change. As such wanted to help her in some way, but I didn't know how! Marriage for me was out of the question. I had seen enough ill treatment of women, by husbands and in-laws and hated young men who made a pass at me. At college once, one of my friends told me that her cousin said it would be fun to kiss Vandna. Instantly she was dropped as a friend by me.

I would have given anything to become a nun. In fact I used to dream of spending the rest of my life, wearing a habit and living in a convent.

I talked to Mummy about her life, and how she felt about being ill-treated by Papa and his people. She opened up to me and told me many things about her life, including her growing up years.

She told me that when she was about fourteen years old, she was traveling with her father and stopped in some relative's place, to have a meal and rest. The relatives had a young man staying with them, who when he saw Mummy couldn't take his eyes off her. Seeing him stare so, Mummy asked him to bring a glass of water for her. Now, in Hindu society a woman never asks a man to serve her in anyway. It is regarded almost like a crime. The young man brought water for her anyway but he had vowed to get even with her someday.

To take his revenge he waited until Mummy was sixteen, and then he approached her parents to ask for her hand in marriage. The marriage was arranged, and they got married and thereafter started the bitter journey of revenge. He paid her back because she had asked him for water to drink. He paid her back throughout her life by every way he could think of, just because Mummy being a woman, had asked him, a man, for a glass of water. He also biased his relatives against her, who helped him to torture Mummy mentally and physically.

When I heard how her in-laws and Papa, had treated her I went to my room and cried. My heart went out to her, and I went back to her and said, "As soon as I have graduated from the University, I am going to get a job. I will take you away from Papa, and all the in-laws that have ill treated you."

The culture did not allow us to show our emotions so Mummy never hugged us or kissed us, neither did we hug her. But when she heard what I said, she reached out and hugged me tightly and said joyously, "I know you are more like a son than a daughter, and you do what you say you would, because you are a woman of your word. I will wait for that day."

When she hugged me it made me cry all the more and made me want to protect her from all the evil she had suffered. I was indeed amazed but also happy at the change in Mummy who had eventually agreed to come away with me leaving her cruel husband behind, something which was unthinkable in a Hindu household or society.

I was determined never to be treated as Mummy or Karri were treated, by anyone. I was turned off from the thought of marriage, and decided to enter a convent and be married to a life in the monastery rather than a man.

I hated it when young men stared at me or made excuses to talk to me. Their amorous behavior annoyed me somehow. I could not stand any man showing any interest in me. This was certainly not normal but that's how I had become after all these experiences.

The sole purpose for my life now was to get a job, earn enough money, leave Papa's house and take Mummy with me, and give her a good and comfortable life, where she could have all the freedom she had never had as a woman. The others in the family did not concern me because they were quite reconciled with Hindu culture, and inhuman traditions, but I was happy to know that I had made a dent in Mummy's thinking and that she was no more inclined to follow Papa, and others blindly.

But was it me who was responsible for her change?

I brought modern novels in Hindi language and some Western novels in English, for her to read, in which she could tell the difference between a proper married life, and the hellish life she was living, where she was treated like an inferior being, or even a slave.

I passed my M.A. in English Literature from the University in my hometown. By then I had decided to live independently and not be intimidated by the men folk in my family, or society. I was furious at the way women were treated in my house by the men folk of the family. We women cooked, served and cleaned, but were never allowed to enjoy life as equal human beings.

I was especially furious when I was asked to stay indoors during the festival of "Holi," which is a festival of colors. "Holi" is a festival when everyone throws color on each other, and has fun in general from early morning till noon. Then they take a shower, change into new white clothes, and visit and greet each other with a hug. Special sweets are prepared and eaten at this festival. We slaved and made the sweets, but were never allowed to throw color at anyone because we were girls. The men walked out of the house in the morning to enjoy with their friends, and came back at noon to shower and have lunch, which was prepared and served by the women. When I was a child I used to be ready with color to throw at people but when I grew up and understood, I never even tried to play "Holi," and resented the festival altogether.

Being independent by nature, I soon found a job as a teacher in a small elementary school, which did not pay much, but this was my first job, a new beginning towards independence. I loved teaching kindergarten kids, so innocent and pure. This first job only paid me 85.00 rupees a month. I gave my first salary to Mummy which brought tears in her eyes. None of her children had earned or given her a penny until now, leave alone giving the whole salary. My giving made a whole lot of difference in Mummy's life. I could see the joy when she spent it on buying stuff for the house.

I got very fond of the kids I taught in this private school. They were so small and helpless. 1 loved teaching them the three R's.

This job gave me confidence to go forward in my quest of finding a better paying job. Mummy was pleased though apprehensive, but she gave me permission to continue in that teaching job. Since Papa was never home during the day, he was not aware that I was gone from home, to work in the school. Everything was hush hush for a few days but somebody from the community went and spilled the beans, and the old boy was livid. This was not done in his house. No daughter of his goes out to work. It was a mockery to his prestige and position in society as a wealthy man!

Well, it was his wealth not mine, so I needed to collect some resources of my own to leave his house with Mummy, and live independently.

He had already shown his displeasure to Mummy, and she had passed the information on to me. Now he confronted me and said with his eyes narrowing, "Since when did you think you can make decisions of your own?" His mouth twitched with frustration.

I was quiet for a while, so he persisted and I replied timidly, "I just want a little experience of working in a school. I don't see anything wrong with it, even Mrs. Simon next door works in a school."

"She is a Christian. She can do what she likes, but you cannot, you have to leave the job, is that clear?"

I stood looking straight at him for a few seconds, and replied defiantly, "No Papa," I said resolutely, though trembling within. "I am not going to leave this job. I have committed myself to teach for at least a year and will not go back on my word."

He was furious, turned red in the face, and stood there menacingly, probably ready to slap me across my face, when Mummy appeared and took me away. Later I came to know that he had raved and ranted about me being rude. He said I was going out of hand, and that I needed a bridle to keep me in check. But probably he was too busy making money to carry out his threat. So I continued working and strangely he never bothered me again about the job.

However, he began cutting down on groceries and other expenses that he took care of. My guess was that he resented Mummy supporting me in keeping my job and my rebellion. He resented any kind of independence for women in the house. Since I did not bow down to his threats he punished Mummy by not giving her money to run the house. In this way he would have control over her, and us. So he stopped giving any money to Mummy when she needed it for the house, probably to teach us a lesson.

Mummy and I came closer and strove all the more to become independent of him. She had started respecting my wish to be independent nevertheless she was so steeped into the Hindu religion that she never encouraged me to convert to Christianity. She never wanted to discuss it. To please her I continued to join her at "pooja" at various festivals, while I kept a look out for a better job and was amazed at my "Modernized Mummy."

We were to learn later, the cause which brought about the change in my mother, and which sadly took away her desire to live.

In the meantime I encouraged Rasna to apply in the school I was serving and luckily she too got a job. So, now two daughters were working while the men folk were looking on helplessly. Since Rasna and I were working, Ragna also joined the rebellion and started looking around for vacancies, but did not want to work for a meager salary, since we were not trained teachers. She wanted to do her teacher's training first, so I paid for her training and as soon as she graduated she landed herself a government job, which paid very well, but she never shared the blessings willingly with us. She gave money grudgingly for the house.

Now all three of us sisters had Mummy's support and were financially more or less independent.

We would notice Papa's revengeful attitude.

Papa showed no compassion and no forgiveness whatsoever, rather he took it out on us where it hurt the most—finances.

But he forgot that he was not god. And God did step in and gave me a much better paying job in a prestigious Christian school, where I found compassion and love of Christ, as I had never experienced before. Here is where I first held the Bible in my hands reverently, the precious Holy Book.

Alfred, the Founder Director of the Educational Institution, started the day with Bible reading and prayer, and that's where I got to read and understand the Bible. It was awesome to be able to read the Book which was forbidden for me to read at home. This job gave me money as well as confidence and dignity with an atmosphere of freedom and opportunity to reach for the sky. It would soon enable me to take Mummy away from Papa and that stifling environment.

Alfred and Kiran his wife, who was the Headmistress of the school, helped me read the Bible. We talked about the different passages we read every morning and they helped me interpret it. They started visiting my home when they saw my interest in the Bible. They were blissfully unaware of the animosity of my family towards the Christian faith. At first every one was cordial towards them. We, except Papa, went for picnics and outings together. But soon it was clear that my family learned that Alfred and Kiran were helping me in my faith journey, and so began to resent their visits.

However, early one morning I was awakened by a flurry of activity and sounds which were very unusual at that time of the day. I shook myself awake, and went to find out the reason of this uncalled for disturbance at that unearthly hour. I found Mummy writhing in pain, with sweat rolling down her face. Rasna was already with her trying to calm her down. I knelt beside her and held her hand. She held fast to my hand and said, "Please do something about this pain." I called our uncle who was a doctor. He arrived and checked Mummy out. He diagnosed gall bladder stones, which needed surgery. He prescribed some pain relievers and asked us to rush her to the hospital for surgery right away.

Papa never showed up, however we got the pain relievers for her. It seemed that Papa was punishing us for challenging him and trying to become independent. So I too did not ask him for help, nor did I ask my brothers for help, and decided that only the women of the house would handle the situation—just to prove our point and independence from men.

I knew where to turn to. Alfred had several doctors in his family and knew the best surgeon in town personally. Kiran would also help while Mummy was in the hospital. In India general hospitals are almost free, but you have to pay for some medicines. Alfred's sister-in-law was a doctor in that hospital. They came immediately, and willingly and took Mummy in their car to the hospital. Ironically my family did not object. I wondered where Papa's prestige was, as the absolute head of the family. What would neighbors say if he did not even show up at the time of sickness.

However, Mummy was operated upon without delay. The operation was apparently successful. We looked after her while it seemed Papa had abandoned her altogether. He never came to visit her, nor did he ask us how she was doing. We began to suspect that there was something more than the eye could see. It was not over our rebellion against Hindu traditions, or male chauvinism alone, that he was distancing himself so, but as Mummy explained that there was another woman he was attracted towards and was seeing her.

She told me that a few years earlier Papa had a friend who died, leaving his widow behind with three kids to take care of. The widow was unemployed, so Papa had started helping her financially and very soon he was having an extra-marital affair. He started giving all his attention to her, and so had no time for Mummy or us. At first Mummy had not understood the reason for his distancing himself from her and from us kids. But one day she went to visit this widow when the kids were in school, and saw Papa and her in an intimate position.

Afternoon was the time for him to be in the shop taking care of his business, but he probably thought being with the widow was a more important business than his shop. Papa tried to make some silly excuse, but Mummy had seen with her own eyes, and things that previously did not make sense, made sense now. She was shattered. That is when she started to rebel against him.

Now that Mummy had seen them together, he became more defiant and began to have affairs with other women. She could not divorce him because it was unheard of, in those days in the orthodox Hindu society.

So she had endured silently and still lived on under the same roof with him. We were not quite ready to be fully independent. Now I understand what had been going on. The old boy was lavishing his time and wealth elsewhere, and so he did not care for us. His affairs became the talk of the town and his prestige went down the drain. This made me more resolute to get Mummy out of the mess as soon as possible. I reassured her that I would be taking her away as soon as she was discharged from the hospital.

A week passed by in the hospital and Mummy was making steady progress. In three days it would be her birthday. So we had cleaned and decorated the house, and got her a very pretty hand embroidered "sari" for her birthday. We were planning a birthday party for her, and had kept it a secret from her. I was elated that we had made it through Mummy's surgery without Papa's help and would soon bring her home. Soon we would celebrate her home coming and birthday.

I had not slept well the night before because our pet dog, a Pomeranian, had constantly howled in a mournful voice. I tried to keep her quiet but she wouldn't stop howling mournfully. I wondered why she cried so.

The next morning when we visited Mummy in the hospital with a change of clothes for her and other things that she might need, we saw three doctors surrounding her. I was immediately apprehensive.

I asked the nurse, "What is going on? Is everything all right?"

The nurse said, "She is bleeding from the operated area."

"But why?" I cried. "She was all right when I left last night. What happened during the night?"

She just looked at me sympathetically and left the room. I dared not ask the doctors, seeing their grim faces. Frustrated, angry and apprehensive of what was happening, I had no choice but to call Alfred and Kiran to ask the surgeon about her condition. They came right away and asked their surgeon friend who was the best surgeon in town, trained in Scotland.

The doctor did his best to stop the bleeding. I saw him working on her but never imagined that she would not come out of it alive. I had never seen death in the family. So it never occurred to me that after a simple surgery by an experienced surgeon, Mummy would die suddenly. We were all looking forward to her coming home to recover completely.

My brothers also arrived in the hospital by that time and Gaurav called our relatives too.

I was confident that when the doctors were done I would get to see mother. But after a little while I saw the doctors coming away from her bedside and so I went a little closer to her. She stretched her hand towards me. I took her hand; she brought it up weakly to hold it. As I did so, I heard her say softly, "Take me home."'

"Of course I will, just let the doctors give you a green signal and I will take you home. In any case you are being discharged day after tomorrow."

The doctors came back, and I went outside the ward and sat on the steps. I thought of all the things we would do for her on her birthday. While I sat there, I saw an aunt of ours coming towards me with a grim face. I thought she was just coming to sit by me.

She came and simply said, "Bhabi is gone," and began crying.

I was stunned and stood there transfixed for I don't know how long, when Aunty spoke loudly, "Did you hear me, Bhabi is dead."

It seemed I had just awakened from a trauma.

Mummy gone! Mummy dead? But wasn't I supposed to take her back home and celebrate her birthday? Wasn't I supposed to take her away and give her a better life? Why did she leave me? Why Why Why? How did it happen?

And that is the last I remembered of the hospital because I fainted. I was taken back home where I regained my consciousness. But I had started a high fever and was still in a state of shock. We had done the best for her. She was progressing steadily, and we were planning to celebrate her home coming and birthday, but suddenly she died.

I could not forget Mummy's plea, "Take me home."

It pounded in my head like a hammer—"take me home, take me home," until I thought my head would explode. That's when I burst out crying and did so the whole night long.

According to tradition, Mummy's remains were cremated and ashes floated down the sacred Ganges River. We being women were not allowed to be at the funeral. At home, I dragged myself from one room to the other, wandering aimlessly trying to figure out what happened.

Why did she die when all was going well? I was so disoriented. Our lives revolved around mother. I had plans to take her away. But God had other plans, as I realized later.

Soon after her death Rasna was married off by Gaurav, to the person Mummy had chosen. Papa refused to show up. I knew that very soon it would be my turn. I had expected it to be after Ragna but that was not to be.

CHAPTER 4

In The Lion's Den

Mummy's death devastated me. *How would I go on without her?*

Above all I was puzzled. Why this sudden and unexpected death?

While her dead body was being bathed and dressed in a red sari, I cut a piece of her blouse, and hid it in my clothes closet. She was dressed in a red sari. According to Hindu tradition, when a woman dies before her husband, she is dressed in red. If she dies after her husband, she wears white.

Gradually I recovered from that shock and fever, but my mind was still blank. I looked at the piece of blouse from time to time, and thought about our shattered plans, to live an independent life. I thought of all the comfort I had planned to provide Mummy in her old age. I thought of all the good times I had imagined I'd have with her, as the years went by. It all came to naught over-night.

Now, the house felt empty without Mummy. During her last days I had become very close to her and I realized that she had started depending on me financially, as well as emotionally. She had become the center of my life.

Some days later I heard that at Mummy's death, all Papa said was, "So, you won. You beat me to it!" Whatever he meant by that remark?

Was he fighting a battle with Mummy? But at that point I did not care. On the contrary I thought Papa had won because he had driven Mummy to her death and left me destitute. He topped it all by moving out of the house and living in another house of his. He also hired a servant to cook for him. Now only Gaurav, Vaibhav, Ragna and I lived in the house—minus parents.

What was I going to do now that Mummy was gone? Would it be worthwhile to convert to Christianity? Would it be simpler to go with the flow

35

*and marry the man with whom my marriage would be arranged by Gaurav?
What does the future hold for me as a Hindu wife?*

There were umpteen questions buzzing in my head. My heart and my
mind were chaotic, and I tried to decide on the right course of action but
was unable to do so. I had lost considerable weight.

After a few days, in the same chaotic frame of mind, I resumed my
duties in Alfred's school. Here I found peace. The atmosphere gave me
a warm feeling of acceptance and warmed my heart, to fill that vacuum
in my heart and life. Alfred and Kiran, often visited and consoled us.
After a few days, I began to understand why God called Mummy away
to Himself. If she was alive, she would never have allowed me to convert
to Christianity. At her death I felt the bottom had fallen off my life, but
now I began to see that as I fell, Jesus was waiting to take me in His loving
arms, lest I dash my foot against a stone, just like in that picture I saw in
grade two at school.

I contemplated on how to go about it. I was nervous but I caught hold
of Ragna one evening and said, "I seriously want to convert to Christianity.
I know you all think I am crazy to even think about renouncing the Hindu
faith, but I know I will be much happier being a Christian, than being
a Hindu and married to a Hindu male chauvinist. I feel rather strongly
and convincingly about being called by Jesus who loves us, especially
children."

She looked at me and raised her brows, but said nothing. I could only
guess what went through her mind. Since we were the only females left
in the house, she knew that all hell would be let loose if she told Gaurav
about my decision. He had now become the acting head of the house,
since Papa had moved out.

Meanwhile, I started taking more active part in the devotions at school
during morning devotions. I could feel that I had become a part of a better
family, each time it was my turn to read the Bible and lead devotions.
Gradually I became more and more convinced of my desire to become
a Christian and that God was calling me. It became an all consuming
obsession and I could think of nothing else.

*If all else failed I would go to my childhood school, convert to Christianity
and become a nun.*

Alfred and Kiran regularly visited us, which made my family somewhat
suspicious of them trying to lure me to Christianity, and they started
resenting their visits. Finally I was asked by Gaurav to resign my job and

stay at home. I suspected Ragna being behind this resignation as she was always the sinister one in the family. So I resigned.

I was forbidden to see Alfred and Kiran, and they were not welcomed in our house as before. I had no option but to do the bidding of the family, because we women had no freedom to make our own decisions. I was virtually under house arrest which made me restless and frustrated, even desperate. I missed the Bible reading and missed talking and learning about Jesus. I also missed my teaching job, which I enjoyed thoroughly. Now I felt that all the joy of life was taken away from me. But I never gave up. The call of the Living God was far stronger than the mute gods of clay.

I started to browse the classified ads in the newspaper every morning. One day I said to my brother, "I need to find work, or I will go crazy stuck in the house."

"Have you decided what job you will apply for?"

"Teacher's job of course!" I said.

"Alright, as long as I know where." Thus, he gave me permission to look for a job, and I started my search.

There were still restrictions on going out of the house. Each time I would have to seek permission to go out, and often I was followed. When not shadowed, I visited Alfred and Kiran. They were an immense source of strength and comfort to me. But they also knew the risk I was taking. So they constantly reminded me to be careful, but continued to guide me in the Christian faith. The biggest question that faced them was—how to have me baptized, without making my family and community angry. They wanted to support me but were at a loss.

Somehow my brother came to know about my secret visits to Alfred and Kiran's house, and I was immediately put under house arrest again. No more job hunting. This time it was literally a house arrest, because I was not allowed to go anywhere. I was not even allowed to answer the door. When I came near the door out of sheer boredom, I knew that someone or the other was watching me from behind the curtain. Ragna was usually the guard on duty. Once, from under the curtain I could see Gaurav's shoes. He had his eye on me as I came out to the front verandah. I felt like a caged animal.

Wasn't Daniel trapped in the lions' den?

One day out of sheer desperation I packed a few clothes in a small suitcase and tried to sneak out. Suddenly from nowhere Gaurav leapt out, snatched the suitcase from my hand, and pushed me back into the room. As he raised his hand to hit me, I kicked him hard in his stomach, which made him withdraw.

My quick reaction, especially the kick not only stopped him, but left him shocked. He couldn't believe it. How could a younger sister, a woman, kick an older brother, a man, now the head of the house? Such behavior was unthinkable and unforgivable in an orthodox Hindu society.

Even I was stunned. It was so sudden and spontaneous.

Gaurav's intimidating tactics had rebounded. The rabbit had certainly turned into a lioness. At that time I did not realize that it was God who had given me the strength to stand up against such brutal treatment and humiliation of women.

After this incident the atmosphere in the house was strange. It seemed as though a violent storm had passed through, leaving everyone in a turmoil. The storm had left me confused. Silence ruled the house, instead of loud Hindi film songs from the radio. I wept with anger and frustration so much that I felt sick to the core, and for the next thirty six hours I neither ate nor drank anything.

Each one in the family remained aloof. No one seemed to care what the other was doing. But they continued to keep an eye on my movements. They were all united against me.

What would they do to me now? I was in big trouble. They would certainly retaliate.

My heart cried out to God for help. Sometimes I could hear the pounding of my heart when I had thought about what might happen, now that things had come to such a head. I could only imagine the worst. They may force me to marry any old fogey as soon as possible. They would do this so that I would not have time to attempt to leave the house again. Once I was married to somebody it would be the in-law's headache. So palm her off to any one who could tame a shrew. I had become a serious problem, and a burden they couldn't handle any more.

I missed Mummy terribly. Had she been alive this situation would not have arisen. I missed talking to her and I missed being hugged by her. On my last birthday she had woken me up with a kiss and a hug. I had never seen her hug the others. She may have started seeing Christ's love in my heart perhaps. We had become special to each other. She too might have renounced Hinduism and accepted Christ as her Savior. But God knew better.

Soon I found a change in everyone's behavior towards me. They became very polite towards me. They even pretended to care for me. I knew their motive was to tackle me in another way. Violence did not work. I wondered what was up! It was long before I knew the reason for such a change in their attitude.

It was Gaurav who came up to me and said, "The young man with whom your marriage has been arranged will be here at 7 p.m. Be dressed properly in those new clothes, which have been placed in your room."

I remained silent but I felt my heart sinking. My family had gone ahead and arranged my marriage with a Hindu man, who was a young and good-looking officer of a bank. He belonged to a rich family, which owned a biscuit (cookies) factory. He was coming to our house that evening for the engagement. I felt trapped, because if I got married to him I would never be allowed to convert to Christianity.

What was I to do? Where would I go to find help?

I kept an eye on the clock. It was a time of intense tension for me and I paced the room in desperation. I could only think of calling out to my Lord and Savior Jesus Christ. I prayed unceasingly until I felt dazed. That's when God spoke to me. I heard Him say, "Come unto Me, all ye that labor and are heavy laden and I shall give you rest."

It was the afternoon of June 30, 1980. I just stood up, He called me over the tumult—loud and clear. At His call I walked out of the house with just the clothes I had on. My mind seemed blank, but I could feel God's protecting arms around me, nudging me to go forward. The miracle was that no one saw me leave the house. I had been watched constantly, but at that moment of crisis God did not allow anyone to watch and stop me from leaving. I was scared to death and kept looking back, thinking that someone might be sure to follow, and drag me back. But no one showed up coming after me, and I was able to get away safely to the main road.

Like Daniel, I had been in the lion's den and none of the lions had been able to harm me. God had sent His angel to protect me. I am reminded of Daniel's words when he answered the King, "My *God sent His angel and shut the lions' mouths so that they have not hurt me, because I was found innocent before Him . . .*" (Daniel 6:22). In my case, the guardian angel shut the eyes of those hawks.

I had lived in that house under the protection of God, not exactly fearlessly but knowing that God would take care of me no matter what.

The decision was mine—either to marry a well-to-do Hindu man or follow Christ.

And so I walked out of the lion's den, unseen and unharmed. I walked fast because running would have made people suspicious. I had no money to pay for transport. I had left my bank books, clothes and jewelry behind. I had even left my certificates and degrees behind, for which I had worked my whole life. And now I was leaving my family whom I loved, in spite of everything, never to return. It was heartbreaking but necessary. It was now or never. But where would I go? I jumped into the first rickshaw and instinctively told the driver to go to Alfred's and Kiran's house, giving him the directions. They would know what to do and guide me. They were influential, resourceful and courageous, with a mission for Christ. I could depend on them.

Finally, I reached Alfred and Kiran's house with a thumping heart. They were surprised but seemed ready to take care of the problem. Kiran gave me a pen and piece of paper and said, "Write to your family and mention that you are an adult and you have the right to choose what is best for you. Mention that you are in good hands, who do not consider you a burden. But don't tell them where you are and ask them not to worry or come after you."

I quickly wrote the note. A servant was sent to my house with the note while Alfred, Kiran, and family and I, drove off to their property, about a hundred kilometers away from our hometown. They had a house in that property, where I could stay while they returned the same night to their own home. They did not want my family to know where I was. They knew the danger that threatened them. My family could have filed a report with the police, that Alfred and Kiran had kidnapped me. All hell would have been let loose. The Indian police is all powerful.

In India conversions are frowned upon but not banned by law, because it is a democratic country. If any person, especially a single girl wants to convert to another religion, she has to do it at the risk of her life. The Hindu fundamentalists do not take it lightly. It sort of becomes a prestige issue for the entire family and the community of Hindus. They would do anything in their power to either bring the person back to the Hindu fold, or even kill them.

When they drove off leaving me behind in the house, reality set in. Until then I was totally dazed. It dawned upon me that I had actually left my house where I grew up, for good! I had fled from an unwanted marriage. What would my family and community say? How would society treat my family now that I had mysteriously disappeared? Would they ex-communicate my family or compel them to get me back by hook or by crook? How would I live alone in a house, on a huge property?

I hoped that the society would not be too harsh on them. They were still my people and I loved them. I did not want them to be hurt, in any way. In my heart of hearts I knew Gaurav was just doing his duty. He wanted the family honor to be maintained by marrying me off honorably to a Hindu. But what happened to the family honor when Papa moved out and left us alone to fend for ourselves? What happened to the family honor when Papa squandered all his wealth on somebody else's children, while neglecting his own? But of course he was a man. He could do anything and get away with it. He had the freedom, but I didn't because I was a woman. I wasn't going to take it lying down. Furthermore, I felt called by Jesus from childhood.

All these mixed thoughts crossed my mind like a flash, and suddenly my eyes filled with tears. I felt completely and utterly alone in the whole world. The truth that I was alone in the building now, hit me hard. I was used to living in a house full of people but now I was all by myself. I quickly turned the lights off and entered the bedroom which had a comfortable looking bed and an oversize couch. Colorful paintings hung on the walls with a picture of Jesus right in the center.

I neither ate nor slept the whole night but kept glancing restlessly around the room. Mixed feelings of fear, and anxiety for the future, and excitement of being independent raced through my mind. I tossed and turned in bed, without a wink of sleep.

Every minute I felt as though someone was trying to break into the house. I listened to the sounds of the night. The cricket sounded louder than usual, the owl hooted rather hauntingly. The soft summer breeze seemed to blow harder than usual. There was a time when I thought I heard distinct footsteps the other side of the door.

Morning came, and I was still wide awake. I quickly went to the window to see if I was safe and saw the servants in the servant quarters, going about their morning chores. I picked up the Bible, read Psalm 91, and felt safe knowing my God who had called me, would not leave me, nor forsake me, though all else may flee. I had some strong tea and prepared breakfast. I prayed and asked Him to forgive me for leaving my family and for my family to have an explanation of my absence for the man who was coming to get engaged to me.

I don't know when I dozed off. I was awakened by the phone ringing loudly. It was Kiran. "How are you, is everything alright? Did you sleep well? Did anyone come? Did you get any calls?"

"I am okay, no one came nor called."

"God will give you strength and guidance for your future. Keep praying and be on your guard. Try to keep a low profile until we know what to do next. As a matter of fact we will go ahead and open a school there, with you as its Principal."

With these encouraging words she hung up.

Principal—I barely had teaching experience. I'd only completed my M.A. in English Literature, did not have any teaching degree, and no administrative experience. But then I'd read, "I can do all things in Christ who strengthens me."

There were times when I felt a wave of loneliness that was triggered by Mummy's death. I missed her all the more because this is what we had dreamed about. Being in a house away from Papa, just Mummy and I, as I promised to give her everything she desired. Regret of not being able to do so filled my heart with sorrow and I wept till my eyes turned red.

This was the time when I realized I had no one to turn to except Jesus Christ. I started praying more and more, rather I talked with Him. Whatever I did, I first consulted Jesus about it, a habit which I have developed. The thought of having Jesus to lean on, gave me immense confidence and peace, since I could never talk to the male members of my earthly family.

So, Jesus became the big brother figure for me and the only male member in my family of two. I loved this relationship with Him and wanted to take on a name which would make me feel closer to Him. Hence, I wanted to take the name Christina.

Days went by and I felt my strength and confidence returning. I had not heard from any of my family members. I wondered what was going on. During the day I craved to go out in the courtyard or in the mango grove and guava grove, but was too scared to be seen outside.

The summer days were hot so I would stay in doors but the cool evenings were inviting, and one day I went to stroll out in the garden. After a few minutes, I felt a queer sensation and the hair at the nape of my neck began to stand. Someone must be watching me. I looked around and saw two women staring at me from behind a bush. My heart leapt. But I did not let them know that I was scared. I casually walked towards the house, out of their sight. I kept a look out until they left, then walked inside the house and locked the door. I never ventured out after that for quite some time. Later I learned that those two women were my neighbors.

Some days went by peacefully. My family apparently took no action but I was on my guard. I knew they would not sit back. The truth was that a whole lot of activities were going on to locate me. They knew I had gone to Alfred and Kiran for help as their servant had delivered my note to them.

Alfred and Kiran remained pillars of strength for me, guiding me and mentoring me. They visited me every weekend and sometimes stayed overnight.

During their visits I started spending time outside, as I loved outdoors. Gradually I started forgetting my anxiety and fear of being discovered by Gaurav and the family. I still missed Mummy and cried often, when I thought of her.

CHAPTER 5

The Missionary

They say that time is the best healer, and our God has plans for each one of us. "Let the dead bury their dead," said Jesus, and "No man having put his hand to the plow, and looking back, is fit for the Kingdom of God."

I loved teaching kids as mentioned earlier, and here I was getting the opportunity to establish a school of my own as its Founder Principal. I was ecstatic. I knew that the Lord had granted me more than the desire of my heart. I was also a little doubtful whether I'd be able to manage to build the project as expected. God had placed a huge property before me, (100 yards x 100 yards), along with servant's quarters. I was further elated when informed that Alfred's missionary friend in England, would support the project. Thus I knew that with God all things are possible, and with that power of positive thinking I put all my energies in building the school. I was happy, because through the school, I could reach out to many with the message of Jesus Christ, just as I had found Christ in my school days when I was a child.

So the next two months were spent in preparing to open the school. We designed flyers and admission forms. We needed to think of the school flag, its name, color of the uniform and design a logo—"In God We Trust." Oh! What excitement! I started going out with Alfred and Kiran to dealers, to have children's uniform made. We named our school St. Nicholas School, because St. Nicks loved children.

The neighbors watched us as we went about in Alfred's car. But by now I had gained confidence, and thought that my family was powerless to do anything against me. We appointed a few teachers and were looking forward to the opening day.

A few days rolled by in the hectic activities of getting the office and classes ready. I had employed a Christian lady teacher, a certain Mrs. Charles, as my assistant, who came to me by reference of someone whom Alfred knew. I interviewed her and found her a quiet sort of a person, but intelligent. I hired her right away. She was also pleasant in looks and speech, which makes a lot of difference in dealing with little ones, and of course with grown ups too.

I had my office right in front of the building. My joy knew no bounds when we got our first admission in kindergarten. The child's name was Nimesh. He was a tiny guy with curly black hair and glasses on his nose. His father was an officer in the Indian Institute of Technology, situated just outside the town. The little child took to me, and hung on to my hand as soon as his parents left. I thoroughly enjoyed his attention. This was a big step towards my independence. Our school was close to the government colony. Soon the officers, including judges and police officials, brought in their children for admission. We had 46 kids within a week—an excellent start.

The journey had begun.

A new chapter of my life had opened up.

There was no question of looking back. Being a small town, and because of the absence of English medium schools, our school soon became very popular. People from different backgrounds admitted their children in our school.

I was very particular about having the Lord's Prayer in the morning, along with our Indian National Anthem. I also had Moral Science as a subject, in which we taught stories about Jesus, along with other religions. No teacher or parent objected to it. As long as the kids learned English it did not seem to matter if I taught the children about Christianity.

Soon I earned the respect of wives of the officers and they started inviting me to be a member of their club. I sometimes visited them, but mostly I busied myself in the school and devoted my heart and soul to bring it to the level that a Christian school deserves to be, worthy of His name.

I worked hard during those early days and loved the way the school was progressing. The school bell rang at 8.00 a.m. and the kids assembled for prayer. Mrs. Charles came fifteen minutes before time. I was in the office by 7.00 a.m. to see that all went smoothly.

We started with the Lord's Prayer which was led by either Mrs. Charles or me, and the kids repeated after us. Then the national anthem was sung, and the announcements or important news of the day was read by one of the students. Then we went in to our respective classes and taught subjects according to the time table. Lunch break was at noon. After lunch we sometimes went on field trips or engaged in some activity like educational games. As the school grew we had to employ more teachers. Most were Hindus, wives of officers, well educated and cultured.

Life seemed good because now I was on my own and was able to tell students about Jesus, but there was always a nagging feeling of insecurity in my mind. I kept wondering about the eerie silence from my family. It was very uncharacteristic of them. I felt the danger within me and remained ready to respond. I never went out alone, only with the kids or teachers. By now my brothers should have known where I was and what I was doing.

The question of my baptism was still gnawing at me and I could find no solution to it. I had approached the pastor of the local churches but after hearing my story they drew back for fear of my family and Hindu fundamentalists. We approached even the missionaries in the area. They were all afraid and said that times had changed.

Alfred and Kiran tried everywhere to find someone to baptize me but no one had the courage. People were just too scared to stick their necks out for Christ. So unlike the early Christians! I was thoroughly disappointed with the Christian leadership and missionaries. Here I was a heathen, who having accepted Christ, renounced the old faith and family, and stepped out leaving the dead to bury their dead, and to give my all at His call. And here were the namesake Christians who turned away from the Great Commission; to reach out and baptize me in His name. Didn't Jesus tell parables to show how there is great rejoicing in heaven over one soul saved, even though there were 99 already there?

Such behavior could have turned me off like Mahatma Gandhi was when he was prevented from entering a white church in South Africa. But my faith in Jesus did not waver. Jesus had called me, not those who said, "Lord, Lord." I knew my Jesus would never fail. So I remained still and held on to Him. I too could have gone back to Hinduism like Gandhi, who was deeply moved by the example and teachings of Jesus, especially the Sermon on the Mount. But due to the evil effect of the policy of Apartheid in South Africa, not only India but the world lost a great soul from entering that church. He was one of the very few who understood the spiritual depth and significance of what Jesus taught, and knew how to apply those spiritual values in this life on earth, especially when Jesus said, "If a man slaps you on your right cheek, turn to him the other also." Gandhi could interpret and deduce what Jesus meant when He said, "Ye have heard it said, 'an eye for an eye and a tooth for a tooth,' but I say unto you, do not resist evil with evil.." (Mathew 5:38-39).

Gandhi not only understood the principles of Jesus' teachings in theory, but practiced them and forcefully implied the truth of love and non-violence in his struggle for India's independence from British rule, upon his return from South Africa. That truth worked like magic. The British handed over the rule as best of friends. In fact the last British Viceroy, Lord Mountbatten, continued to serve India, after independence on August 15, 1947, for another six months as India's first Governor General.

Gandhi would have possibly converted to the Christian faith, had they not turned him away from entering that church because of the dark color of his skin. As a leader of the independence movement, and respected as the spiritual Father of the Indian Nation, he would certainly have influenced others on his team, and many other freedom fighters as well, to consider accepting Christ, as he had proved the effectiveness, and meaning of Jesus' profound words when Jesus said, "I am the Truth, the Life and the Way." Gandhi had proved it so, by walking in the footsteps of the Master. Gandhi could not understand how anyone claiming to be a Christian and worshiping Jesus, a colored God Incarnate, could be color prejudiced? He couldn't accept the logic of racism.

Be that as it may, I decided to continue and follow Jesus, and was not going to be deterred by any human element, black or white, brown or khaki. I was determined not to look back having put my hand to the plow. If I did I wouldn't be worthy of His Kingdom. I would stand firm on the promises of my Savior, though all else would flee—which they did—from the wrath of man. They could not see the wrath of God! My Jesus was a Living God, and I knew He would take care of me and any problem in my faith journey, as He had done so far.

Alfred and Kiran were great pillars of strength at a time of suspense like this. Their solid faith in Christ was infectious. They said God's way is the best way, though mysterious, and His timing is perfect always, if only we put all our trust in Him.

And sure enough His response came unexpectedly as one sunny weekend, when Alfred and Kiran were visiting, and we were enjoying our afternoon tea, sitting on the porch, a stranger turned up. He limped a little, wasn't very tall, and was quite insignificant to look at.

Introducing himself he said, "I am Rev. Subhan, the new pastor of the Methodist Church, at the other end of the town. When I heard that a Christian school had been opened recently I decided to visit you." Then he looked straight at Alfred and said, "You may not remember me, but I remember you and your whole family. Years ago, when we were very young, and when my father was pastor of the Methodist Church in our hometown, and your father was the lay leader who preached often, then I used to know you. Your mother played the organ and your sister and you made up the choir in that church. Our families often visited each other . . . ."

Alfred interrupted him and said, "Yes, I remember your father, he was a convert from Islam, the name Subhan did ring a bell when you mentioned it. Though I do not remember much of that distant past, nevertheless, I am pleased to meet you after so many years, since our childhood. I do recall that your father went about on a bicycle, and then he bought an old motorbike that made quite a noise . . ."

However, after some pleasantries Alfred mentioned my story, and how I'd left home and family to convert to Christianity, and how the Christian leadership was so afraid to baptize me. He listened very attentively and we saw angry expressions, passing over his countenance now and again.

When Alfred finished he said, thumping his chest, "I will baptize her, in fact I will have our Bishop come over and baptize her, and celebrate the occasion as never before in this town."

We thanked Pastor Subhan for offering to get me baptized by the Bishop of the Diocese of Lucknow, and expressed our appreciation upon his courage. Being a son of a convert himself he understood the whole situation quite easily, as his own father had gone through somewhat similar experience. That insignificant little man was directed by our God, as a spiritual colossus to solve the problem of my baptism, and with grandeur.

So once again, here was the mighty hand of our God, stretching out, protecting and lifting me up in the midst of despair. Our God is faithful, as wrote St. Paul in 1 Cor. 1:9—"God is faithful, by whom you were called into the fellowship of His Son Jesus Christ our Lord."

And I became part of that divine fellowship by being baptized on November 15, 1981. May the Lord bless that little man, Rev. Subhan, wherever in the world he might be today.

When the ceremony of my baptism was complete and my name became Christina, I bravely sang my favorite song, "Take my life and let it be consecrated Lord to Thee." Alfred accompanied me at the piano accordion.

I meant every word of the song. Finally 1 belonged to Jesus legally and no one could take Him away from me. I was part of His family and my heart's desire was fulfilled. Now I was ready to go full steam ahead and take an active part in the church. After the baptism service, we had a huge party of celebration, where we invited all the Christians of the town and parents of children who belonged to various other religions. I'm sure there was great joy in heaven too, as we celebrated on earth.

As mentioned above our school was located on a large piece of land, with guava, mango, custard apple, sycamore, jackfruit and tamarind trees on three sides. There were many birds and animals there. The front of the building had an open ground, which faced the main road.

Nature always fascinated me. The beauty of nature always gave me the joy, which comes only from the excitement of knowing Jesus, through whom all things were created.

I loved the huge mango trees whose roots reached deep into the soil and clung tenaciously to the ground, bearing the extreme weather of Northern India. I loved to climb the mango trees and enjoyed eating the ripe and juicy mangoes, the first fruits of the season, straight from the tree. When I climbed high on the trees I felt closer to God. I would sit up there on a high branch, musing on the blessings of God bestowed upon me.

I have always been a lover of nature because my father owned a huge farm where he planted many crops. During our summer vacations we used to visit that farm and were thrilled to climb trees and be out in the lap of nature, in my growing years.

The guava grove was not as inviting as the mango grove, because the guava trees were smaller and slippery, while the mango trees were reaching up high and were safer and more fun to climb. The ground was covered with grass. A variety of creatures lived in the underbrush such as rabbits, peacocks, monkeys, hawks and above all poisonous snakes too, mainly cobras and vipers. It was my Garden of Eden!

The amazing grace was that none of those animals ever tried to hurt us, or the students. On the contrary it was I who went swiping those snakes with a hockey stick, whenever any strayed in the building during those years. Strangely, never did any snake attack, or bite any of us. In fact they ran in the opposite direction as soon as they saw me come after them. How did they know? At such moments the words of Psalm 91 always came to mind. I could feel the presence of His protecting arms about me and the school. If any snake ever bit a single child, all the parents would have withdrawn their children in no time. The Hindus worship the cobra as "Naag devta," a god. They also hold a festival known as "Naag Panchmi," when they feed snakes by leaving bowls of milk where snakes often appear. The next morning those bowls are found empty. But do snakes drink milk? Has anyone ever seen them do so?

There is another belief that there are certain Naags (cobras), which can transform themselves into human beings at will, to protect their worshipers when necessary, and back to their original form when the danger was over. They are known as "Ichcha Dhari Sanp." However, I was still in danger, living alone and surrounded by cobras. But even though surrounded by such creatures I never saw a single cobra transform itself into a soldier to protect me!

One bright sunny Sunday morning, the doorbell rang. I was always nervous on weekends when there was no school and I was alone. I wondered who it could be on a Sunday morning but opened the door, since I was still accepting admissions. Two serious looking officers of the law stood at the door, wanting to question me regarding my conversion. My baptism was still recent, and the news of my conversion had spread far and wide through church magazines.

When I learned the purpose of their visit, my heart began to pound so hard that I found it difficult to breathe. Probably the shock of being interrogated by officers of law, when I was alone frightened me so. I was born and brought up in a family with no history of ever being involved in any police investigation, and here I was facing two officers who were questioning me as though I had committed a crime.

They told me that somebody had reported that I had been converted to Christianity against my will. With my heart pounding, I heard them out while I sent a quick prayer to God. Suddenly I felt His presence and safe. No "Ichcha Dhari Sanp" appeared to protect me! Both officers were Hindus and I could see contempt in one of the officer's face while the other continued his questioning, which made my flesh quiver with indignation.

I told them about my background and qualifications and how I came to know about Christ. I told them how I had wanted to become a Christian from an early age, and how my efforts were thwarted by members of my family. But now that I was an adult, and since we had freedom of religion in India, I converted willingly. No one had forced me to convert. No body converted me against my will. Someone had made a false report. I had not broken any law by converting to the faith of my choice, I told them.

I looked straight into their eyes and asked, "Do you think with my upbringing and educational background, I could be forced into conversion to Christianity against my will? You have just talked to me; do I appear to you as a weak human being, who could be lured into changing my religion, without knowing and understanding what I was doing? You believe in God, does anyone have the power to change your faith from Krishna to Christ, unless you yourself believe and convert?"

The two officers looked convinced that I was in no way forced or lured into conversion from Hinduism to Christianity.

There was a relaxed atmosphere thereafter and we were able to talk about the school and the progress it was making. They told me that my school had a good reputation in the community in spite of the resentment over my becoming a Christian. They said the parents of students in my school, were full of praises about the education we provided. Their children were eager to attend school, which is rare. Most children cry and refuse to go to school.

With the atmosphere relaxed I took this opportunity to tell the officers about my joy in accepting Christ—a God who loves and cares for us. Not like other gods who judge and punish us according to our "karma" (deeds). Jesus forgives our sins. No other god does. I had sown the seed. Even though I was nervous and scared, nevertheless God gave me the courage to talk about Jesus. They left satisfied.

This incident had shaken me no doubt, and when the officers left, I went straight to my haven—the mango grove. I sat under one of the trees, looking at the wild flowers, and thanking God for the opportunity to tell other pagans about Jesus and the difference He had made in my life. I had never been through this kind of interrogation which left me shaken. Yet I thanked God for the opportunity to clear my position and bring the non-believers to the knowledge of Christ.

I sat under the tree quietly for a long time, gazing at the flowers and grasses, dancing with the breeze, and soon my heart too began to dance with the lilies of the field. I had won my first battle against two officers of law by the grace of God.

I do not remember how long I sat there, but soon I started looking further than the trees, and noticed the sun shining on the dew drops on fallen leaves giving them a beauty that only God could create. I sat looking at the beautiful colors and the bright sunshine, and considered as to which color was matching my mood?

I looked at several flowers and picked the brightest red. This reminded me of blood. The thought of blood took me to Christ's crucifixion and the blood He'd shed for the remission of my sins. I was ashamed that I was distressed at a small interrogation for accepting Christ by two mortals, but Jesus was betrayed, tempted and treated as a common criminal by Roman law. Christ, who is the Son of God suffered for me. His precious blood was shed on Calvary so that we could have eternal life abundantly. Jesus took all my burdens away. No god of clay could take it away from me. O how much He cared for me. I felt so much lighter within and without.

I knew God was in control and with that knowledge came great calm. I was rejuvenated in my faith, and picked myself up after having fallen from the acne of delight to the nadir of despair. I now believed that this visit of the law had a purpose and that it was God's will. He was viewing me through the lens of grace, which protected me and equipped me with answers. My part in this was to accept humbly whatever He plans for me and believe that He will always be there with me, to save me in time of crisis. It is not we who are fighting; it is God Himself who is fighting for us. I felt much richer, fuller and deeper in the love of God, than I had ever felt. I had learned that it is better to be on God's side. He is a friend so true, and will always be with you all the while. I never had any agents of law bothering me thereafter. My victory in Jesus was complete. My journey as a missionary for Christ had begun.

CHAPTER 6

What In The World!

"Madam, Poonam is dead," said one of the students casually. I looked up from my file of papers, on which I was working in my office, early one bright morning in July. I had a lot of work to catch up with, and the kids began arriving at school. It was 7.30 a.m., and since my mind was so pre-occupied, the news of Poonam's death did not quite register.

But when another student, who lived nearby, came crashing in my office, and almost screamed, "Madam, madam, Poonam hanged herself last night," it was then I realized the seriousness of the tragic news.

I was dumbfounded and asked, "Why in the world did she commit suicide?"

I hurriedly closed the office and rushed out towards Poonam's apartment, wondering all the while how she could have done this to herself when she had so much to look forward to.

Poonam was a young, recently married woman, who had come to live in the apartments behind the school with her husband. She was rather slim, and no one knew why she looked so forlorn and lost. We came to know later that she was being mistreated by her husband and was expecting a baby in the near future.

I reached her house which was swarming with policemen. There was already a crowd gathered outside. I walked straight in to her apartment and the sight took my breath away.

Poonam's lifeless body was hanging from the ceiling, well dressed in a colorful sari and her face as calm as though she was asleep. Her feet were touching the low table, which she had supposedly kicked off. I had never seen a suicide case before, but even my inexperienced eyes could see that the table had not been kicked away by Poonam, instead her feet touched the table. I suspected that it was another case of dowry killing—a murder by the husband and mother-in-law, and made to look like a suicide case. Probably she was poisoned first, and then hung. Policemen, being Hindus, know facts and condone dowry deaths, and no serious investigation takes place.

The husband and in-laws pretend to weep and wail. In some instances professional mourners are hired. I was extremely disturbed and infuriated with the husband, in-laws and police, and was so grateful to our God for having called me away from such a pretentious culture.

For no fault of hers, a young life had been taken away, all for lust of money. Looking at her hanging there, I wept in my heart for that beautiful life cut short.

My flesh quivered with indignation against such murderous traditions in a so-called civilized, educated society. Women are indoctrinated to go quietly to their death by the hand of their husbands because men are supposed to be their god. As such, women would attain "moksha" (Salvation), if killed by their husbands. What kind of logic, or tradition is that where money was worshiped as goddess Laskshmi, and where human life had no value whatsoever? How true are the words of Jesus that you cannot serve God and mammon together.

It was obvious to everyone present that it was murder but nobody took any action, not even the police, as most belonged to that faith. Even the girl's people believe that their daughter attains life eternal and freedom from "Avagaman" or cycle of re-incarnation. No longer would she struggle through her karma to achieve salvation. Another bride burning custom which still lingers on in certain parts and communities of Hindus is called "Satee." An inhuman ritual according to which, if or when a husband died before the wife, the widow was burned alive on the husband's funeral pyre. They believe that the woman was a demon who had devoured the husband. So burn her. Something like the witch burnt in Europe in Middle Ages. The Mughals (Muslim rulers) tried to prohibit the practice, and the British tried by law, but Satee still lingers on in remote communities of Western India.

Imagine the socio-psychological effect upon children who lose their mothers to Satee or dowry killings. Some witness the latter more than once in their families. After a few months we heard that the husband of Poonam had re-married, and of course received another dowry to fill his own family coffers.

So, the murder is to acquire more wealth in dowry, at each successive marriage. This was the religion I was born in. I was disgusted and depressed for months, and could not feel normal for quite a while.

What in the world was this religion worth, which teaches and promotes murder of women for easy money, actually blood money? What is any society worth where women are treated like property or burden which can be disposed of at will, and with impunity?

Hinduism was originally known as "Arya Dharma." (Dharma meaning religion). So Arya Dharma meant religion of Aryans. In pre-historic times, the sub-continent of India was populated by a race known as Dravidians, and Tribals, who are dark skinned and speak strange languages. Later, a combination of Indo—Aryans, Indo—Europeans and Celts, invaded India through the Khaibar Pass in North Western India and occupied that part, driving Dravidians far North East, and South. The ethnic divide is quite marked. In due course of time, the Indo-Aryans got browned off in the hot sun of the plains of North Western India, and speak very different languages, and brought in Arya Dharma.

The Muslims from Asia Minor when they invaded and ruled India in the Middle Ages, gave Arya Dharma the name of Hinduism, and the country Hindustan—"the land of Hindus."

Unlike Christianity, Hinduism believes in millions of gods and goddesses. It begins with the creation of humanity from one of their gods called Brahma. The absolutely unchanging factor in Hinduism is the basic principle of caste, which according to them means that some human beings are inferior to others by birth. They believe that the highest is the priestly caste, called **Brahmins** or **Pundits;** who came out of Brahma's head, and are the intellectuals and priests, Pharisees, if you please. From the chest were created **Kshatriyas** or the rulers and warriors. From the thighs came **Vaishyas;** the traders or the industrialists, and lastly from the feet were created the **Shudras;** the unskilled workers or the scheduled caste who are also known as "untouchables," who do all the menial jobs for the higher castes, like washing, cleaning or disposing of dead bodies etc. Gandhi gave Shudras the name of "Harijan," meaning people of their god Hari or Vishnu.

These four main castes are the very basis and structure of water-tight Hindu society. As time developed these four main castes were divided into hundreds of sub castes, depending on the occupation of the community, e.g. tanners, sweepers, cremators etc. During the Mughal rule, a new class or caste of Hindus known as Kayasthas was created. It would take reams and reams of paper to describe each one of them.

According to the Hindu faith, the people came from god Brahma and had to work their salvation (mukti) by their own good deeds or works, known as "karma." This philosophy of karma is closely related to, or intertwined with the doctrine of re-incarnation according to the Hindu belief.

A person is born into a particular caste according to his/her own deeds, or misdeeds of the previous life. If one has been a good person, then according to one's good karma, one would be born in a higher caste, and thereby would climb up the ladder of caste system and would be born finally as a Brahmin, with a real chance of achieving union with Brahma, the Absolute, if he has been a good Brahmin. Thus he is released from the cycle of re-incarnation or "Avagaman," and achieves salvation. Conversely, if a man's karma is bad, he goes down the ladder of caste system and into the animal kingdom. That is why Hindus are not supposed to kill and eat meat.

The literature of Hinduism is found in several books known as the Vedas. There are four of these. It is said that in Vedic times, women occupied a position of respect, but with the distortion of the belief in reincarnation, people started believing that to be born a woman was due to a curse because of a sinful former life.

The second way to salvation is through complete devotion to the god Krishna, as the sole object of worship. Since there are so many gods and goddesses in Hinduism, the individual picks and chooses a favorite god or goddess to worship. This god whom they choose is known as the "Ishta devata," whom they may worship at home as well as in the temples dedicated to that deity.

Hinduism as I know, basically believes in three main gods. The head god is called Vishnu (god the father or protector), the second is called Brahma (the creator god or preserver), and the third god is Shiva, (the destroyer). Vishnu is regarded as the Supreme Being, the god of gods; of whom the other gods are manifestations, such as Krishna and Ram and others. Each god also has a consort, who is a goddess. Vishnu has Lakshmi, (goddess of wealth). Brahma has Saraswati, (goddess of learning and music). And Shiva has Parvati, (has two aspects, Parvati the benevolent and Kali, the blood thirsty).

As mentioned earlier, one of the incarnations of Vishnu is Krishna, who had several wives and concubines. He is even known to overcome the multi headed snake demon, "Naga," and subdue him by dancing on the serpent's heads, with women looking on admiringly. He is known for his flute playing, which makes the maids or "gopies" gaze rapturously at him, and finally give their all to him. Another incarnation of Vishnu is Rama. Krishna has proved to be a more popular incarnation than Ram, especially among women. However, Vishnu's spirit supposedly moves over the waters in the lap of multi headed cobra, and he comes in the form of human beings or animals into this world whenever the human cup of sin overflows, according to Indian mythology. Vishnu has been incarnated in the form of a turtle, a fish, the god Ram and the last incarnation, Krishna.

Krishna treated women as possessions, and had millions of wives. Wherever he went, he just picked up women for his harem. There is a story that as Krishna was walking down the road one day, he saw a woman who was ugly and bent double with age. He went towards her and held her chin and pulled it upwards. The woman was at once transformed into a beautiful young girl, and followed him to be his concubine.

There are millions of other gods and goddesses, whom the Hindus have absorbed from other ancient cultures down the ages. They seem to have a problem with Christ as they equate Him with Western civilization.

Another set of Hindu books is called Purans. The life and agony of Ram is found in another book called Ramayan, and finally the most important book is the Bhagavad Gita, which is the sermon of Krishna in the midst of the battle of Mahabharat. It is in this Bhagavada Gita, that Krishna expounded his philosophy of "Karma" and ironically, non-violence, having initially instigated Arjuna to fight and kill his kinsmen, the Kauravas, by opening his mouth and showing the battlefield of the dead after the war.

Hinduism is one of the most ancient religions of the world. In India idolatry, black magic, child sacrifice, witch craft and other rituals are widespread, including numerous superstitions.

The Ramayan, the religious book of Hindus, was originally written by a man called Vyas in Sanskrit, and translated into Hindi language by a "woman hater" named Kalidas, who probably started the trend of subjugation of women in the Hindu society. The story is that Kalidas was separated from his wife for a long time, and so when he felt an urgent sexual need he walked for miles and miles, and then swam across a river at night to reach his wife's house. He climbed up what appeared like a rope, that was hanging from her window, only to realize later that it was not a rope, but a snake. He had climbed on to a poisonous snake to reach his wife, in the heat of the moment. When he related this incident to his wife, she reprimanded him for his extreme sexual need. She rejected his amorous advances and sent him packing.

Thus rejected, he felt like a jilted lover, and was enraged. He became a woman hater thereafter. This hatred for women he later translated in his story towards the end of Ramayan, when Ram turns his wife out of his house for no fault of hers, which the Hindu men lapped up gladly to suit their own purposes. Thus started the subjugation of women to the satisfaction of men.

I had employed a Karate teacher in my school, who was a Hindu, a Brahmin. He had a delicate and beautiful wife, and a four-year-old daughter. He also lived in the same apartment building as Poonam. One morning we came to know that his wife had committed suicide by swallowing rat poison. It did not make sense because she really loved her daughter to the point of obsession, and she would never have dreamed of leaving her little child alone in the world. I somehow could not believe that she had committed suicide. But her body had already been removed and cremated. There are no funeral homes in India.

I knew the man was having an affair with another younger and more modern college girl, whereas his wife was an uneducated village woman. I knew that this was also a murder case, like the death of Poonam, and the man had simply exterminated his first wife, for another marriage and dowry. I felt helpless and frustrated. I did not know how I would deal with the man when he came to school. I could not forget the dead woman's face, whom I had met several times when she was alive, and whose precious life was cut short. If only she was a Christian, she would never have met this fate.

People in India are misinformed that Christianity is a European religion. However, Christianity in India is as old as Christianity itself. It was brought to India in 52 AD when St. Thomas established the first church in the Southern most tip of India nearly 2000 years ago, and established what is called the Syrian Church today. This church has two denominations now which are called Mar Thoma, and Jacobite. St. Thomas came to India when many of the countries of Europe had not even heard of Christ. Unfortunately those early Christians of Southern India failed to spread the Gospel and kept it to themselves, being rather shy.

St. Thomas preached the Gospel all over Southern India, especially in Kerala and converted many to Christianity. He established churches in seven towns. In Kodungallur, Kottakkavu, Palayur, Kollam, Kokkamangalam, Niranam and Chayil. It is also known that he frequently visited Malayattoor hills for prayer. Later on he preferred to go to the east coast of India, to Madras, or modern Chennai, where he was martyred in 72 A.D. by a fanatic Brahmin priest. He is buried near Madras. His tomb is preserved to this day, and is known as St. Thomas Mound. There are still some Syrian Christians in South India.

A new era dawned in India when Vasco de Gama from Portugal discovered the sea-route to India rounding the Cape of Good Hope. Vasco de Gama landed on the West coast of India, where he established the colonies of Goa, Daman and Diu, under the Portuguese flag in 1498.

The King of Portugal began sending traders and Roman Catholic priests to evangelize India, and established several Roman Catholic churches in and around their colonies in due course.

Christianity really spread in India and the Far East when British East India Company established its rule in the sub-continent of India, and the Far East by the Regulating Act of 1773 and Pitt's India Act, which set up a Board of Control responsible to the Parliament of Britain in 1784. Earlier, in 1534, King Henry VIII had declared himself as the synonymous Head of State and the Church in England, breaking away from the authority of the Pope in the Vatican in Italy. Ever since then the Monarch of England has also been the Head of the Church of England, or the Anglican Church, a Protestant Movement. So along with the East India Company and the rulers came the Church and its missionaries. The greatest British missionary was William Carrey, who came to India in mid seventeen hundreds. Between the British government and missionaries, they established many churches, schools and many other charitable institutions.

Gradually Indians also converted to Christianity and Christianity became a dominant religion in British India. William Carrey landed in Calcutta and established over 200 schools and hospitals in Bengal. He brought the first steam engine to India, established the newspaper Statesman, the printing press etc. he did more for India than any one man ever did. As such the Indian postal department prints a postage stamp on

December 6 to commemorate Carrey's services to Indian people. December 6th is also St. Nick's Day. Both St. Nicks and Carrey loved children.

Even though St. Thomas brought Christianity to India as early as A.D. 52, nevertheless, the church was confined to the very southern corner of the peninsula for centuries. It was only with the British rulers and other European missionaries that Christianity spread in a big way across the sub-continent and other parts of S.E. Asia. It was not surprising therefore, that the people of India considered Christianity as a religion of the West. Later Switzerland, Australia, and New Zealand came to strengthen the notion that Christianity was a white man's religion—whereas Jesus was Jewish, an Asiatic.

Before independence, Hindus, Muslims, Buddhists, Jains, Sikhs, and Parsees, even agnostics and atheists, men and women of various ethnic groups, shapes and color, lived quite peacefully. The British had united the sub-continent into one nation, given us English as one common language, to communicate and work in harmony. They'd taken all the Rajahs, Nawabs, Chieftains, land-lords, and other petty rulers throughout the land under their wing, and stopped them from fighting amongst themselves, or to rule as dictator within their territories. The British were far sighted, sent out the best men to rule and educate Indians. These officers had to qualify and pass a very tough examination, known as the Indian Civil Service Examination in England, before being sent out to run the affairs of India on principles of justice and democracy. They industrialized India, encouraged both private and public sectors, built railways, roads and communications, and legal system. They taught Indians to develop their own skills. In short they brought India out of the Stone Age, and set her on the path of modernization.

Their uncanny favoritism towards India was beyond compare. They called India a "Jewel in the British Crown." I don't know why, but they considered India as a special asset to their Empire. In 1834, they sent out a man named Lord Macaulay, who had become a member of British Parliament four years earlier. Macaulay was a brilliant historian, writer, poet and administrator. His book of poems called "Lays of Ancient Rome" was prescribed as an integral part of English Literature, in all British schools in India, and the rest of the British Empire.

When Macaulay landed in Calcutta, Bengal, he looked about and said, "Now let us educate the people of India in such a way that they may be able to run their own affairs one day." He knew British couldn't rule

India or hold on to their empire forever. Thus, as mentioned earlier, he introduced what he called the "Filtration Theory," in Education, whereby he would educate the "classes"—the elite of India, and allow education, or knowledge, to filter down to the "masses." That thereby India would learn the principles and values of democracy, freedom, equality of opportunity, justice and liberty etc. they not only taught these values but practiced them themselves. Whenever any governor of the East India Company, or any other British officer acted in an unjust manner, he was immediately called back to England, indicted, and tried in the court of law, and if found guilty was punished. The case of Warren Hastings, and Jallianwala Baagh are famous examples.

However, besides other reforms in the Indian Educational system, Macaulay introduced the study of the New Testament, and teachings of Jesus, for the education of the heart, and character building, to emphasize the love of God, and neighbor, which enshrines the Ten Commandments. Also the Lord's Prayer, and how to learn to forgive those who hurt us, just as Jesus did from the cross. Those of us who went to such churches and private schools, got a taste of it. Macaulay's reforms worked like magic. Everyone was happy without being in pursuit of it, like running after a mirage.

Maybe that's why I rebelled against the injustices, and criminal practices, and atrocities against women in the faith of my fathers and was drawn to Christ, and converted to Christianity.

Dr. Stains, the Australian missionary, who was serving the lepers in India in about 1998, was burned alive with his two sons when they had gone to a leper's house to give him medicine. The Hindu fundamentalists said he was converting the villagers to Christianity. His wife was left alone with a teen age daughter, who decided to stay on in India, and continue her husband's missionary work. She also said that they had forgiven the people who had murdered her husband and sons in ignorance.

It was in such a hostile and anti-Christian environment that Jesus called me. And I just walked out of my home, with only the clothes I was wearing. I left everything I owned, to follow His call, with no regrets. I remember that day so vividly, and I have never looked back, having crossed the Rubicon.

I am glad I decided to follow Jesus. I'm glad I left those gods and goddesses with feet of clay, and walked away from Krishna to my Christ, when He called. I'm glad I walked away from the indignities of that culture that condones dowry killings, Satee, and subjugation of women. I'm blessed to have shaken the heavy yoke of that karma for the cross. And during these last thirty years, I have walked with God from day to day. Having put my hand into His, there is no turning back.

I left the old world behind me, and came empty handed to follow Jesus and taste of His amazing goodness and grace. The blessings and joys I experience with Him are beyond measure. I can hardly stop counting my blessings. From the bondage of sin I have come to freedom in Christ. He's a friend so true. He keeps all His promises. I have first hand experience of His love and care.

When I am faced with any problem and wonder, what I should do, Jesus solves it all and opens another door. All I can say now is that it's fun to be a Christian, and as a great American missionary, Dr. Stanley Jones asks with tongue in cheek, "And it gets funnier everyday—doesn't it?" It cannot be explained. Walking with God is an experience—beyond compare. As they say—the taste of the pudding is in the eating of it. O come, taste and see how good the Lord is! "Blessed is the man who trusteth in Him." (Psalm 34:8)

CHAPTER 7

The Persecution Increases

The progress of the school was spectacular. I had hired a Dutch lady, wife of a rich Indian executive, as a teacher, which brought prestige to the institution according to the Hindu social norms, where "Lakshmi" (goddess of wealth) or money is worshiped.

I had employed a woman by the name of Shanti for cleaning the school, and gave her a place to live on the school campus. Her family also lived with her. She had two daughters and two sons, who also helped.

I started teaching her kids the English and Hindi alphabet, and then admitted them in the school free of charge. They were over age for the class, but still I worked hard with them by teaching them after school and bringing them up to the required standard. Since they belonged to the untouchable or schedule caste, they had never been allowed to attend school. I took care of them as my own kids, clothing them, feeding them and taking care of the whole family.

It became my mission to teach the academically weak, and the untouchable kids in the evenings, free of charge and worked hard to bring them to the level required. It gave me immense happiness and satisfaction and a sense of accomplishment, to know that these children passed the yearly exam, and were promoted to the next grade. I provided them with books and stationery because they were too poor to buy any.

I did this because Jesus said, "Let the little children come to Me," thereby showing me the way. There was a lot of resentment among the Hindu teachers because they had to touch the untouchables, but they needed the job, so they stayed on. But since childhood I sided with the meek. Being a tomboy, I used to beat up the boys who bullied the weaker kids in my class.

One evening one of the poorest students, Ajay, whom I coached in the evening, came and said, "Madam, my Mummy has sent this for you because you don't take any fees from us."

Saying this, he handed me a bottle of mustard oil and some salt. I was quite touched and said, "When I have not asked you for fees why did your mother ever think of sending this? This is unnecessary."

His face fell. So I accepted that bottle of oil and salt.

How could I refuse such a gift of love? I felt extremely moved at this act of sacrifice and gratefulness, but compensated it by providing new clothes to the children later. Later Ajay graduated from school and went to college. When Ajay grew up and got a job in the Indian Navy, he came to visit his Alma Mater. He was taller than me now. We have a tradition in India that the students touch their teacher's feet, and Ajay visited us several times, and never forgot to touch my feet, despite the fact that he had a prestigious job as an officer in the Indian Navy.

On my birthday in 1983, I was all by myself and suddenly in the evening saw Alfred and Kiran drive in. They came and said that I needed to go with them and that it was an emergency. I tried to ask them what emergency, but didn't argue and went with them. We came to an unknown house and we all went in.

"SURPRISE!" they yelled as we entered the house. It was Mrs. Charles' house and this was a surprise birthday party for me. There were no other invitees, only the Charles' family. I was so touched to get this surprise of a lifetime. It was very different from the house I'd left behind. Here I felt loved, especially Christ's love, surrounding me.

Days went by, and I was becoming less watchful and went into the orchard without hesitation. I climbed trees, played with the servant's kids and was quite off guard. Because of security reasons I had bought a Pomeranian, which was very intelligent and fiercely devoted to me. Her name was Sherrie.

One afternoon just after school, Shanti's elder daughter came to me.

"Madam, there are two people standing outside your office. They want to see you."

I went to the office and saw two strangers standing at the door, blocking it. Immediately the hair at the back of my neck stood on end. They were both tall and strong. One of them was rather stern looking, with hawk's eyes. I felt strange in my stomach and knew they were not parents come for admissions of their children. It was clear that there was something wrong, but I tried not to show any fear on my face. I talked to them calmly and could feel their blazing eyes on me. They were not concentrating on the conversation; instead their eyes darted from left to right. They were trying to take a quick look around the office. In spite of the fear I felt, I remained calm and polite, even though my heart thumped so hard, that I felt it would pop out of my body.

"What can I do for you? Do you want to admit your kids or have you just come for information?"

"We are just looking around for a good school for our kids."

"Well . . . ?"

At this remark they both looked at each other and the stern man nodded to the other. I was absolutely alone in the office at that time and I could have easily been subdued by the two men if they attacked me.

Suddenly Sherrie came bounding and snapped at the visitors. She went for one of the men's foot. He tried to kick her off, but she kept attacking him. The men were rattled and backed out. As soon as they were out, I slammed the door on their faces and locked it. Then I went to the window to see what the men did. I was shocked to see a jeep parked on the road near the gate, with Gaurav, my brother, sitting at the wheel!

So this was their plan. Gaurav had brought these two ruffians to kidnap, and take me back home, and to the Hindu community.

I felt faint with fear and apprehension for a few moments.

If Sherrie had not come to my rescue, I don't know what might have happened. It would have been quite easy for them to gag and pick me up and force me into the jeep. I would have been helpless. There was no one to help me. I was soon on my knees thanking God. Once again God had saved me from a threat that I would not have been able to handle without His help.

I called Alfred and Kiran and told them about this attempt and they were alarmed and concerned.

"Do you want us to come there?"

"No, I just called to tell you what happened here, but I am fine. God is taking care of me. Please don't worry. I'll inform the Police Superintendent (Sheriff) who lives close by. He will arrange for my safety."

That night I could not sleep properly. This had taught me never to be off guard. But how careful can one be?

Besides luxurious cars and taxies, India has an extraordinary system of public transport. There are buses, railways, airways, three wheelers with engines, and three wheelers pulled by men, known as rickshaws, also horse driven vehicles known as "tongas" and "ikkas" and bullock carts. All these are used for public transport. We had a number of rickshaws to bring the children to school. One morning I saw a crowd of people gathered at the gate, and one of the rickshaw pullers talking loudly and throwing his arms around. There were several parents surrounding the rickshaw puller. I was puzzled and I called Shanti's husband.

"Go to the gate and find out what is happening," I said.

He came back with an angry look on his face and refused to say anything.

"What were they talking about?" I asked in a raised voice.

With a little difficulty he uttered, "They were talking about you."

"All right, what were they saying?"

"The rickshaw puller was saying that you were a Hindu and you had run away from home to become a Christian. He was asking the people to withdraw their kids from our school." I was amazed, as the rickshaw driver was one of my employees.

"You mean that rickshaw puller who came begging and I gave him a job?" I asked in a shocked voice. "What has come over him? Bring him here."

When the man went to get the rickshaw puller, I tried to figure out what was happening and then it struck me that when kidnapping did not work, they were trying to bias parents to shut the school down by other devious methods. They were using the servants to spread false rumors about me, so that the parents would pull their kids out, and the school would collapse. The rickshaw man refused to come to the office and disappeared from the scene. But my relatives did not stop there. Some Hindu parents did get biased and began to complain against my staff, particularly against Mrs. Charles. One of them said, "Mrs. Charles is my daughter's teacher and I feel she is not teaching properly. My daughter has learned nothing. She never checks her home work etc. etc.

To which I replied, "I evaluate every teacher's work, as well as the children's progress regularly, and find her work quite satisfactory."

"Well, your Mrs. Charles talks to the kids in class about your leaving home and family to convert to Christianity, instead of teaching," she replied looking straight at me.

Oh God, when will this end? I thought. *Will I ever be able to run this school in peace? Why can't they leave me alone to decide upon the faith of my choice?*

To the parent I said, "I will look into the matter."

The next day I called and confronted Mrs. Charles, who herself was a Christian and asked her about the accusation made against her. Even though she denied it, I could not trust her. She was an enemy within, so I had to let her go.

Nevertheless after a few days, I saw her and her family visit the house across the road. The people living there were landlords, rich, with enough money and all the time in the world to create mischief in the neighborhood, and delight in it as a past time.

Shanti's family had become like my own family and I took care of them likewise. The kids were all over my house, watching TV, and reading the books I had, including Bible stories. Even their parents and friends sometimes came to chat with me. Now Shanti had started working part time for the people across the road. I did not know them personally. I'd heard that Mrs. Charles and the rickshaw puller, were both seen visiting that house and realized what was going on.

Gradually I started noticing a change in the attitude of Shanti, and her husband also. They stopped coming as frequently to chat with me, and were often quite rude. I was doing for them what no one had the courage to do. I had lifted them up socially and admitted the children to attend classes with higher caste children, which is against Hindu philosophy of Karma. No one ever thought of educating them. Because of their own "karma," or bad deeds in previous life, they were born in that lower caste, and had accepted their lot. To be born in a higher caste in the next life, they would have to do good "karmas."

Then one evening I saw the rickshaw puller, Shanti and her husband and the people who lived across the school, gathered outside their house, and talking amongst themselves.

So, this was the reason for the change of attitude in the servants also. That meant that the family across the road had been approached by either my family, or the Hindu fundamentalists, or both. These neighbors of mine were my enemies who were causing all the trouble. That house became the headquarters where my enemies met, and planned and plotted evil against me, and the school.

The next morning I called Shanti and her husband, and fired them, and ordered them to leave the campus immediately.

I could see surprise on their faces. They then realized that they had lost all the privileges given. They knew they were guilty and left the following day, without a fuss.

Once again I was all by myself on the huge property, and vulnerable. So far all attempts to turn parents, teachers and servants against me backfired. But now I had to be more watchful what they'll plan next.

For a couple of days I cleaned the school myself. I needed to replace the servants and only scheduled caste would agree to do the cleaning work.

There was a village about twenty kilometers away from the school. One of the laborers who had worked for the school building and who had shown an interest in the school, lived there. I decided to pay them a visit and bring the family to work in the school, to replace Shanti's family. This couple had three daughters and one son. The eldest daughter was 24 years old and unmarried, due to poverty.

Once again I took on the responsibility as a parent. The first thing I came to know about them was that the couple was suffering from tuberculosis. I immediately took them to the hospital and had them treated, paying for all the medicines. I also provided breakfast for both of them, while they were recuperating, and made sure that they ate it all. They were soon healed completely. The man was fond of liquor, a habit which I detested.

The family pitched in and did the cleaning work, and I paid each one of them for their services.

Soon I started teaching the younger girls. They had never been to any school. The youngest was admitted in the school and she joined the group of kids for extra tutoring in the evening. Later I taught the kids how to open bank accounts and save money. I had started them with the Bible stories too.

The eldest daughter wanted to help more so she asked me one day. "Could I cook for you? It would give you more time to devote to the school."

I thought about it and said, "Alright, but I will teach you how to cook the kind of food I like, and will pay you extra."

So she started cooking for me, and gradually I started depending on her to do all the kitchen work. I gave her permission to help herself with whatever she needed from the kitchen, and take the left-over's to her family.

Two years passed peacefully, the youngest daughter proved to be a good student and was doing well in school. The second daughter was not so bright, so I admitted her in the sewing school and she was being trained to be a tailor.

These sewing schools had mushroomed as cottage industries, and were run by housewives in their homes. Women in the lower strata of society were not educated enough to get jobs, so they taught sewing to girls in their homes. Girls who could not afford to go to expensive sewing schools, enrolled in these classes. This was convenient for poor people who could not afford to send their kids to expensive colleges, where they were trained to make designer clothes. In due course the girl could open her own tailoring business and be self-employed. The eldest daughter was way beyond marriageable age according to Hindu standards, so I started looking around for a prospective groom for her.

Meanwhile my health began to deteriorate. I felt I did not have the same strength and energy I used to have. Very often I felt sick in the stomach and wanted to throw up. Months passed and I began to wonder why? The brightness on my face diminished, and there were shades of grey under my eyes. I was completely baffled as to the cause. I had never had any health problems before, and God had blessed me with extraordinary energy. I could work for hours without feeling tired. Before the day was over I felt quite lifeless.

Am I overworking myself or is it stress, I wondered.

Puzzled, I decided to see a doctor. He ordered a few tests and asked me to come the next day.

"Who cooks your food," he asked me, "do you cook yourself or do you have a servant?" I was puzzled.

"I have a servant girl who cooks for me." I said.

"Bring a sample of food that has been prepared by her, and do not tell anyone."

Not knowing what to expect but wondering why he asked for the sample, I took it to the doctor the next day. He asked me to come and get the results the following day. What a shock of my life I got.

I was being given slow poison! Somebody was putting a small dose of arsenic in my food and I was blissfully unaware. I asked the doctor to keep this information confidential because it would be bad for the school.

Now I knew why the girl never took any left-over's.

I called Alfred and Kiran and told them the situation. They were appalled and came over to the school right away.

"How are you? You look quite pale," said Kiran.

"I am more angry than sick now. How ungrateful people can be!"

"We have to think of a way to move these people out of this campus because these people are dangerous. Remember they are of the lowest caste, who have criminal tendencies, and it would be a problem to get rid of them, because of new laws in their favor," said Alfred with a worried look on his face.

The new law passed by the Supreme Court of India, said that the scheduled caste could not be removed from their homes, under any circumstances, or fired until indicted and proved guilty.

"I will think of a plan to deal with them, but for the moment I will cook for myself," said I.

1 could tell that Alfred and Kiran were worried.

When the daughter came and offered to cook for me, I looked straight at her and said that the doctor had asked me to be on special diet, which I could easily prepare for myself.

"I can make the special food for you," was her reply.

"No, thank you. I can easily manage that."

I asked her to leave me alone because I was feeling unwell and wanted to rest. I lay down in bed and talked to Jesus for quite a while, and asked Him to give me the wisdom to understand how people can do such things to harm fellow human beings.

A few days later I felt much better and renewed mentally, but physically I was still quite shaken. The doctor had given me some medicines to purge my system of the poison, and regain my strength.

Meanwhile I was making plans to get rid of the family who was threatening my life.

I had stopped the daughter from cooking and finally got her married off; thus the family lost all the privileges from the kitchen and also other benefits. They were quite frustrated. Encouraged by the mischief mongers across the road, they began to get aggressive. I was at my wits end and turned to the Lord as usual when in a jam. Hasn't He said "Come unto me all ye that labor and are heavy laden, and I will give you rest?"

Once again He came to the rescue. A new senior police officer got his children admitted in our school. When I mentioned to him about the aggressive and threatening attitude of the servants, he at once saw that my life was in danger indeed, and took immediate action.

The following morning he brought in his posse of eleven officers, and charged the family under Indian Penal Code for attempted murder! The punishment for the offence is seven years imprisonment, not simple, but rigorous imprisonment. Knowing what seven years of R.I. in Indian jails could be, I asked the officers not to charge or arrest them, but just get them out of school campus, which they did.

Once they were out, I was again without servants to clean the whole school. I contacted a few parents who helped me find a janitor, but this time I refused to give living quarters to anyone on school premises. The new janitor came in the afternoons, finished her work by evening, and left. I paid her monthly and maintained a distance from her due to the previous bitter experiences. The police officials provided me ample security, as most had their children studying in our school. The "guru" or teacher commands great respect in Indian culture and parents go out of their way to do things for their "gurus."

I kept thinking of ways to show God's love to the people of that town and I came up with a plan. Every Christmas I had a grand party planned for the people who were willing to come. It was like an open house and started in the morning. The biggest class room was chosen, and I set up the big room with Christmas decorations and prepared all the goodies myself, except the Christmas cake. Christmas cake in India is a specialty of Indian Christians. It is a fruit cake and has a special recipe which is absolutely delicious and unique. I had the Christmas cake baked in a bakery by professional bakers.

This open house was like a mission to me. It took me days to plan it. The first year I had to send out invitations, but by the second year word got around that there was a Christian school which had open house on Christmas Day, and everyone was invited. So people of all castes and creeds especially Hindus, poured in. It was a great opportunity to bring people to the knowledge of Christ by pictures, scriptures and tableaux.

The first guest arrived as early as 7.30 a.m. I wasn't even ready. But I was happy that word had got out, and people would understand the love of God and why He was incarnate in Jesus to save us from sin. The Hindu knows the concept of divine incarnation as Krishna, Ram and other gods are incarnates of Vishnu their Father God. I had a Christmas tree as well as the manger scene in one corner of the room. I knew people would come in and ask about it, and I would be able to answer their questions. Above all I could high light the difference between the purpose and teachings of Jesus and other gods, and hoped to bring others from Krishna to Christ and from Karma to the Cross.

Our first guest was an officer in the civil court. I had never seen him before. He had brought his children with him and all of them had a great time visiting, hearing about the story of Christmas and enjoying the cake. With the Christmas cake there were various Indian Christian dishes that I had learned to make from cook books.

The continuous flow of people to the open house never stopped till late at night. I must have served hundreds of people, friends, acquaintances, and strangers. I did this for many years and hoped that the seed that I was sowing would bear fruit one day, by the grace of God.

Now the school had grown considerably. One morning I saw a short woman in white approaching me when I was outside with one of the classes. I took her to the office and offered her a chair. She said, "I want to admit my daughter in your school. My name is Mrs. Sharma."

"How old is your daughter?"

"She is six years old, and is already studying in Central School, where 1 am a teacher."

"Why on earth would you want your daughter to be admitted in this school when she is already studying in Central School?"

She looked innocently at me and replied, "Because I have heard of the good reputation of your school, and that it is based on Christian principles, which builds character as well. I want my child to learn about God and His laws."

I was puzzled because admission in Central School was rather difficult for mediocre children.

This woman was a teacher in that school; therefore, she could secure admission for her daughter therein. It was a privilege which this woman wanted to forsake? Why?

Central Schools were established by central or federal government of India and are regarded as Chartered schools. There is a tough entrance exam. Even the parents are interviewed to assess if they could match the school standards at home. Though puzzled, I handed her an admission form to fill. By her name it was evident that she was a Brahmin, the highest caste of Hindus. I also noticed that she looked at me with piercing eyes, as no other parent did.

"Bring Diksha tomorrow morning to school at eight o'clock sharp, Mrs. Sharma." With these words I ended the interview.

The same evening Mrs. Sharma was at my door again with her daughter. Diksha was a pretty six year old, with two pigtails of jet black hair and light complexion. She had a pretty dress on and seemed to be intimidated by her mother and shy of me. I talked with Mrs. Sharma for a while and offered her a cup of tea, as the custom in India demands. Weather being pleasant, we sat outside and chatted while Diksha went off to the swings. Mrs. Sharma then started asking me rather pointed questions about my background, which I considered a little odd.

They left after a while and I got busy with my work. However Mrs. Sharma became a regular visitor to the school. She was a widow, (which explained her white clothes) and so brought her child to school as there was no one else.

As time developed, and with her regular visits, we became quite friendly. Probably my lonely existence made me welcome Mrs. Sharma's friendship without any suspicions. But Satan is rather persistent, and one day Mrs. Sharma invited me to her house for her daughter's birthday party. I had decided not to go to anyone's house or to a private party. I went to public programs where there was safety in numbers. Mrs. Sharma had shown her concern and friendliness and lulled my suspicions, and so I promised to attend the said birthday party.

I drove down to her house and knocked at the door. She welcomed me in the living room. Diksha was nowhere to be seen; neither were there any guests. I had brought a birthday gift for Diksha. The living room was small and crowded with knick knacks and the doors of the adjoining rooms were shut. I felt shut in and a little apprehensive, but said nothing. The woman came and sat beside me.

"Where is Diksha? I want to wish her happy birthday and give her this gift."

"She will be here soon," said Mrs. Sharma, "You are a little early."

I waited for Diksha and the other guests but there was no sign of anyone. Instead, after a time of silence, I noticed Mrs. Sharma staring intently at me, and then she asked, "Why did you convert to Christianity?"

"Because I wanted to, what made you ask and where are the other guests?"

Smiling she said, "I have to make an offer to you. We will give you all the money you want, a big house, and a very rich man as your husband."

"Why on earth would you do that? I have not asked you for these things?"

"I will give you these things if you agree to return to Hinduism."

Shocked, I stared at her speechless. I still did not quite comprehend the seriousness of the situation. Suddenly it dawned on me that this was a set up! I was invited here on a false pretense. There was no birthday party. It was to get me to this house where they could corner me alone. I looked at the door and found it was bolted. I knew full well that I was trapped.

This woman had betrayed my trust and friendship and done what my enemies had asked her to do. Namely try to buy me back and bring me back to the Hindu fold or . . . .

The hair at the back of my head rose, but I did not show my fears and retaliated angrily, "What makes you think I would want to return to Hinduism? And why would I accept any man you have in mind as a husband? Do you think I am incapable of finding a husband for myself? Do you think I am a pauper that I would accept your offer of monetary gains and a big house? I have left all that behind." By now I was almost at the top of my voice. This response made her a bit nervous, but she stood her ground.

"If I want worldly goods I would never have renounced them and can still get them without your help. Do you understand? How dare you talk to me like this?"

Instead of answering Mrs. Sharma pursed her lips and stared at me.

While showing my anger I gradually walked towards the door, quickly unbolted it and stormed out, jumped into my car as fast as I could; and hit the road.

How dare she think that I would leave my Lord for money or for a rich husband?

On reaching home I thought about the situation and how I'd walked into the trap unthinkingly. While I was still pondering, the phone rang.

"Hello." It was the woman Sharma.

"You got away this time but next time you will not be as lucky," she threatened.

"There won't be a next time." I retorted firmly. "We live in a democracy, with freedom of religion, and I am an adult. I could get you in trouble with the law. If I were you, I wouldn't try—so forget about your next time. You won't win, no matter what you try," I said.

But she continued saying, "It is not only me, there were many others in the house. I had *a pandit* (Hindu priest) and several others who wanted to convince you."

I shuddered. *O my God, why did I ever accept her invitation and go there alone?*

I slammed the phone down on her. I had been stupid but our God understands our weakness and rescues us.

Why can't they leave me alone?

I had been running the institution for several years now, and found no reason whatsoever to return to the old faith. Instead by now my faith had become deeper and stronger.

I thanked God for protecting me once again from a situation that was beyond my means to escape from.

Next morning I was back in the office ready to face challenges of another day. Then I saw her coming! The woman in white! Mrs. Sharma was coming towards the office. My heart skipped a beat, but I braced myself for the worst. She did not enter the office. On the contrary she told one of the teachers that she was withdrawing her child. I heaved a sigh of relief and prayed I'd never see her again. The Lord took care of that. Mrs. Sharma was transferred to another town, far, far away. I have never seen or heard from her ever since.

A few years went by without any such incident. The students and the staff were loyal to me and the school. The school building was slowly becoming inadequate for the large number of kids being admitted. School resources were not enough to build any new classrooms. So, we planned to raise funds to add four more class rooms. Donations came pouring in and soon the foundation was laid, I stood and watched with joy as the walls went up.

One afternoon, after school was over, there came a visitor. He was from the court of law and had brought summons for me to appear in court, to explain how I was constructing new classes without the approval of the blue print and following the legal procedure? Fortunately I knew the District Judge, and discussed the matter with him and how to solve this new threat. He advised me to have the upcoming walls and foundations removed overnight, and he said he'd try and have the case dismissed. It broke my heart to see the construction being torn down, all donations wasted and to crown it, we had to spend more to bring the walls down.

Our hopes fell from the acme of delight to the nadir of despair. But God had seen us through other problems.

I was absolutely scared of court cases because I had never been involved, nor had the time or money to waste. I called Kiran and Alfred and told them what had happened. They revived my hopes by saying, "Maybe God has other plans. His timing is the best. His way is the best way. Sometimes we fail to involve God and go full steam ahead in our enthusiasm." They were right. So I learned to wait upon the Lord, to consult Him, and seek His guidance.

CHAPTER 8

The Light Shines In The Darkness

Kiran's health began deteriorating and her family was very worried about it. She was beginning to lose her memory and weight. We started wondering what was wrong with her, when she could not remember even our names. She used to wander around the house and forget what she was looking for. It was pathetic to see an intelligent person like her, who had done one M.A. from India, and another from the United States, and was the Headmistress of a big school, losing her memory.

After many tests and regular visits to the doctor, it was diagnosed as Alzheimer's. We knew there was no cure in India for Alzheimer's. We were all at a loss and genuinely concerned as to how to take care of Kiran. She had lost her job because she could not work any more. We all did our best to care for her as long as we could.

We prayed about it and decided that Kiran could live with me as I could hire a separate servant to take care of her while Alfred was all by himself.

India does not have facilities for Alzheimer's patients, neither are there any retirement homes for senior citizens. Family members have to do the needful. So, I looked after her as best I could. I hired a servant exclusively for her who took care of her when I was at work. Kiran was gradually getting worse, so much so that she did not know how to eat. We used to feed her by hand, and bathe and dress her. It was difficult and stressful but we managed somehow. Those days were some of the most difficult for all of us. To see my mentor and guide declining so fast was heartbreaking. But I could not do any more. We just had to do our best and pray.

The family that lived opposite the school, openly laughed at us. The enemy seemed to be winning and I asked God why He was allowing it. I thought of the story of Job.

One morning during my devotion, I read Psalm 3 which said "I will not be afraid of ten thousands of people who have set themselves against me. Arise, O lord and save me, for Thou hast smitten all mine enemies upon the cheek bone, Thou hast broken the teeth of the ungodly." And that is exactly what God did. That night not long after, the chief of enemy was going on his motor cycle, drunk as usual, when he crashed head on in—to the solid railway barrier. He was literally smitten on his cheek and broke most of his teeth in that accident. He had to undergo several painful surgeries. But after a few months, he was back again, mocking as usual, and conspiring against the school.

With Kiran's illness and never ending vigil for her, I was at my wit's end. I prayed unceasingly, but it seemed God had turned a deaf ear. I was certain God had a plan in mind for me, though I did not know what, at that time. About a year passed with a patient of Alzheimer's in the house, and I wondering all the while how to handle the situation. Just then came the answer. The Roman Catholic nuns, Mother Theresa's Sisters of Charity, had opened a nursing home, in a town nearby and it was decided to admit Kiran there. She died peacefully a year later.

We were all devastated but life went on for us as usual. My enemies knew full well that I was discouraged and vulnerable. Years ago I had lost the only support I had when my mother died, and now Kiran's death really made me feel quite forlorn. But what could I do? I just had to go on forging ahead, because if I let my feelings get the better of me, the enemy would be quick to take advantage of my vulnerability, and strike. So, I had to put up a brave face. When we trust and obey the Lord, the worst brings out the best in us. My condition was no comparison to Job's. I was going to walk and not be weary, run and not faint and believed that all things worked together for those who loved the Lord through thick and thin. He had never forsaken me in the past, and I could trust my future in His loving hands.

I continued to pray and take care of the school as usual. I took the children on educational trips, to see ancient churches and historic places in other towns, especially the Neo-Gothic Anglican Cathedral in Allahabad, and Nehru Park etc. and they seemed to be very interested in the history and background of churches in India. I hoped that all those trips would somehow turn the children's hearts and minds towards Christ.

I was also amazed at the years that had gone by, without any personal harm to me or the students. God had protected us through all the changing scenes of life. Being single I was quite vulnerable in the male dominated society of India. Nevertheless didn't Jesus say, "Are not two sparrows sold for a farthing? And not even one shall fall, without the Father knowing it. Or be forgotten. Ye are of much more value than many many sparrows before God, even the hair of your head are numbered. Fear ye not therefore, my heavenly Father watches over you." Thus no matter what happened, in God I continued to trust, and the words of that beautiful song—"His eye is on the sparrow, and I know He watches me," rings in my heart, as I write this. Thus I remained a witness before people as Jesus had also said, "Whosoever shall confess me before men, him will I confess before my Father who is in heaven." (Mathew 10:29-33).

CHAPTER 9

A Ray Of Sunshine

An unmarried woman in a society, where women seldom stay single, is scary, especially when Kiran was no more. My heart felt heavy, being human, and in moments like these I turned my eyes upon Jesus and read Psalm 121.

Alfred visited me more often now. He was nervous about my staying all by myself. Two years went by and we went about our business as usual and whenever Alfred visited the school, I learned much from him as he had the best of British education, and had studied in the States. Furthermore he had held administrative positions in several countries. He had experience of establishing many educational institutions in India and abroad. He had been in the English speaking lands twice over, from Canada to New Zealand, and it was delightful to hear and learn from his rare global experience, which few have.

One afternoon I was particularly despondent when I heard Alfred's car honking at the gate. I was surprised because he had not called to tell me of his visit. I was happy to see him anyway.

"What a pleasant surprise! If you had told me, I could have prepared lunch for you."

"I had lunch before coming. Thank you anyway. I keep thinking and worrying about you and I have been praying and God has answered my prayer. He has shown me the way."

I waited to hear what Alfred was getting at. He beat about the bush and wouldn't come out with what God had to say. For a moment he was lost in deep thought and then with much chivalry he proposed, "Would you marry me? I would not be worried sick about you once we were married. It would be the best solution"

I remained silent for awhile. The thought of marriage was new to me, what with my Hindu background. But Alfred was different. He was kind and gentle, never belittled women, full of humor, and above all he had brought me to Christ and protected me, cheered me up when I was downhearted.

"I know we have age difference but I assure you that you will not regret it. They say it is better to be an old man's darling than to be a young man's slave."

"No, age is not a factor, I just did not think of marriage. It is too sudden. I had always thought I would never marry. I had always wanted to be a nun. I need to pray about it."

When Alfred left, I prayed to God to guide me in this important decision of my life. I had mixed feelings of nervousness and excitement when the words of God in Genesis 2:18 came to mind, "And the Lord God said, it is not good that the man should be alone, I will make a help mate for him." I realized that marriage between man and woman is God's plan for us. He created every living being male and female, blessed them and said, "Be fruitful, multiply and replenish the earth."

The idea of becoming a nun seemed contrary to the Creator's design and purpose. That thought came to mind as a result of Hindu customs. Men in that society had distorted God's plans and trampled upon women's rights. Being intolerant towards injustice, I wanted to escape from marriage, because of the treatment meted out to women in that dark culture. But Alfred was a Christian. It was a very different culture. He followed Christ. Jesus treated women with great respect, love and dignity. He even sent out two, to preach the Gospel. His first two pastors, or missionaries were the Samaritan woman at the well, and Mary at the tomb after His resurrection.

It began to dawn on me how gentle and kind Alfred was towards me. All fear and prejudice against marriage began to see the Light of God. It was not good for either Alfred or me to live alone. I began to realize that God was opening a wider door for me, for greater service to propagate the Gospel in the world, in order to bring others to the love of God, and accept Jesus Christ, as their personal Savior, and Lord. God was showing me the way once again. I recalled why and how God made it possible for me to walk out of my house, and from a Hindu marriage. How, so suddenly, He's called Mummy away, whom I loved above anyone, to Himself. It seemed rather cruel at the time, but if she was alive, I couldn't have left her or the home to accept Christ, and would certainly have felt condemned to marry a Hindu, quite against my will and suffer the consequences thereof. The thought made me shudder and sent a chill down my spine.

Furthermore being of rebellious spirit and of very independent nature, I would constantly have been at loggerheads with any man, who'd force his will on me or mistreated me as Mummy was, and my sisters and other Hindu women were. We'd have gone hammer and tongs at each other constantly. There would have been no peace at home. It would have been hell on earth.

The more I thought of Alfred's proposal, the more I felt the Hand of God therein. God was speaking to me in His still small voice. He was guiding me. Even though Jesus said that in heaven they neither married nor gave in marriage, nevertheless, I felt that God did arrange marriages. He brings about the right circumstances, but leaves the decision to us, and never forces His will upon us.

So I decided to enter marriage arranged by God, my heavenly Father from heaven, rather than that which was arranged by my earthly father and was being forced upon me against my will. I knew it was a miracle of love that God protected me that day, when I walked out of the house on June 30th 1980, from that arranged engagement with a Hindu, and from misery. No one in the house saw or heard me leave. They were watching me like hawks constantly and had prevented me from escaping earlier. But, in His perfect timing God shut their eyes and ears, to save me, just as He shut the mouths of lions, to save Daniel.

Yes, God had saved me from that triple headed Hindu lion of clay, for a purpose and it was He who was opening doors for me all along. How could I say no? This would be a turning point in my life. Now the decision would entirely be mine, for better or for worse. Alfred was so different. Besides being well educated cultured and refined, he was a godly man. His parents were missionaries and so was he. He was also very talented and was a pillar of strength for me. Could I ask for more? Who could encourage and nurture me further in my Christian faith?

Since Kiran's death Alfred had begun to visit the school more often, and gave valuable advice and directions wherever necessary, and introduced singing, which the children enjoyed immensely. He knew all kinds of limericks and community songs and made the school ring with melody divine. His visits brightened up the school. It was fun when he came around and we began to look forward to his visits eagerly.

Shouldn't I open the door of my heart and accept God's plan or purpose for me, and say yes to Alfred's proposal? I witnessed miracle after miracle taking place in my life. I ought to listen to and obey the Lord's voice without fear, and take this next step in faith. He would make things work for the good, from better to even better, for those who love Him, as life went by.

But being a woman, and an Indian at that, who grew up as a tom boy, and never had a boy friend as such, it was hard to say yes to Alfred outright. So, I thought of teasing him. Trying to look serious I said, "Alfred I cannot marry you."

He stared straight at me and said "Why not, what's the problem?"

"No problem."

"If there's no problem then . . . ."

He seemed a little puzzled, but when he saw me chuckling and looking askance, he understood that I was playing hard to get, and stretched his arms towards me, but I ran away. In his dignified way he followed me and held my hand, and put the engagement ring on my finger. I hardly knew how to respond, so I just stood still, looking at the beautiful ring, with my heart thumping away strangely. He then put his arms around me and kissed me gently.

When I was in school I thought of becoming a nun, not a wife!

Alfred left after a while, saying that he would call me after he had discussed the marriage plans with his favorite sister.

We got married in the Methodist Church, with his family and friends attending. I had no family member present, as I could not have them for fear of inviting trouble. However, I was convinced that I had done the right thing and had God's sanction and blessings on our marriage. Together we would serve the Lord better. God had given me the very best man to love and to cherish until death us did part. That age difference is an added advantage in our life. I began to see the wisdom of being an older man's darling. Alfred can understand me and my problems more sympathetically than any other person. If ever I got angry at him he never retaliated but told me some story like, "Once upon a time the young lions were having a stag party," he'd say in a matter of fact way. "Well they noticed a mouse also dancing amidst them, and so one of the lions asked the mouse, 'hey what are you doing here?' The mouse replied 'I too was a lion before my marriage."

Sometimes when we argued he'd say, "I'll always have the last word." I'd say, "Oh yeah? And what's that?" I would ask. And he'd say, "Yes dear." His humor with tongue in cheek is incomparable, so is his patience. Never has he spoken harshly, never ever have we had a blow up. I'm convinced I did right in the sight of God, beyond any reasonable doubt.

Soon after marriage, Alfred and I felt the call to full time ministry. But the question was how and where? What about the expenses? It seemed like an impossible dream, but deep within us we believed that with our God all things are possible. (Luke 18:27). These are the words of Jesus who went on to say, "Verily I say unto you, there is no man that hath left house, or parents, or brethren, or wife, or children for the Kingdom of God, who shall not receive manifold more in the present time, and in the world to come life everlasting."

How profoundly true! It leaves me absolutely astounded. Every single syllable of that amazing grace and assurance stunned my senses. I had not read those words when I left my house, family and friends, when I walked out of my house empty handed, with only the clothes I had on, to follow Christ. I could now shout from house tops, how I had received manifold more in this life, and shall receive life everlasting with Him, in the world to come, in that New Jerusalem—the Holy City of God, prepared by Him.

O, trust in this Lord, leave the sinful world behind and come, "taste and see how good the Lord is," to them who trust and follow Him; as I have, and continue to do so. I assure you that the Holy Bible is the written Word of God, and Jesus is that Word Incarnate, who is coming again to gather all His faithful ones unto Himself. Yes, the King of Kings shall rule the world forever and ever. And of His Kingdom there shall be no end. Thus it is written, that it might be fulfilled. (Luke 21:22). Come unto Him and He will fulfill the desires of your heart. (Psalm 145:19). Didn't Jesus promise, "Seek ye first the kingdom of God and all these things shall be added unto you." (Mathew 6:33). No book of magic can give you a better formula which works wonders like the Word of God. We have heard the above words so often that we have taken them for granted. But I know from my personal experience of the past that you can trust the Lord in all things and He will take care of you, come what may.

Psalm 62:8 says "Trust in the Lord at all times, ye people, pour out your heart before Him: God is our refuge." And Proverbs 3:5 emphasizes the fact saying, "Trust in the Lord with all thine heart; and lean not unto thine own understanding."

Those who printed, "In God we trust," on the U.S. dollar, knew well the significance of the above words, and must have had first hand experience of the blessings and joy that trust brought to this great land, a nation under God.

And we know that our God is faithful, and called us to the fellowship of His Son Jesus. (1 Cor. 1:9). And so Alfred and I poured out our heart's desire before Him to open a wider door for us to study His Word further, and prove ourselves worthy to serve Him further according to his Great Commission. (2 Timothy 2:15).

We'd had experienced how our Lord had seen us through safely in the past, through all the dangerous scenes of life, from the moment I'd left my people and renounced idol worship. We knew we could trust our future in His loving and caring Hand. Unless the Lord opened the door and guided us in, our labor would be in vain, and the words of Psalm 127 rang in our ears. The Lord was telling us to be still and know that "I AM GOD."

Through past years in my walk with God, and now alongside my beloved husband, I knew what God inspired in us, He would faithfully fulfill beyond our imagination. If only we allow Him to lead us.

We didn't have to wait long. Things began to happen in His mysterious ways. An alumnus of Bethany Theological Seminary, who taught school under Alfred, and whom he had helped with visa formalities etc. years earlier, and was now a U.S. citizen, came to visit us and suggested we consider seriously to enter Bethany Theological Seminary, and that she would do all to sponsor us at her end.

Imagine our delight, we fell on our knees and thanked God for opening the door, but once more there was another hurdle looming before us. It would cost us a pretty penny to get to the States and the Seminary in Richmond, Indiana, and to settle in. We'd need money for books and stationery and few other miscellaneous expenses. We realized it would be to the tune of at least a hundred thousand rupees, which is quite a large sum in our currency, and which we certainly didn't have, nor could raise unless we sold the extra land, with the guava grove we didn't need for the school. But before we could do that Alfred's sister gave him two hundred thousand rupees—just like that. She was an American citizen, retired and returned to India. She knew we were planning to study in the States so she advised Alfred to continue serving in India, as he had been to the States twice and other countries and seen those far away places, with strange sounding names. She asked him to serve his own people. To this Alfred replied, "And who are my people? My people are those who love the Lord." The call of God was stronger. But the strange thing was that being opposed to our leaving India, she still gave us twice as much as we needed to get across half way around the globe.

God and His mysterious ways are beyond our understanding. But God hadn't done with filling our coffers. Kiran had left about two hundred thousand in her provident fund, which was added on. Furthermore Alfred had his provident fund and gratuity, and I had my life insurance money refunded to me. Money galore just began pouring in from everywhere. We were literally inundated under His "showers of blessings" as says Ezekiel in chapter 34:26. It was a demonstration of love so amazing, so divine. Amazing still are the words of Jesus, when in Luke 18:27 He says that he who leaves his home and family for the Kingdom of God, shall receive manifold more, in this life here on earth. Not ten fold or a hundred fold, but manifold more times here. How true! By now we had nearly a million rupees, which is quite a large sum. (Incidentally, one dollar was worth eleven rupees in those days). Had we sold the orchard land, we could have had another half a million.

Enter Satan, complete with horns and barbed tail, to tempt us. "You both can live comfortably for the rest of your life in India on the interest this large sum will fetch, which would be more than ten thousand rupees per month. Why do you want to slog? At your age you need to relax." But Alfred and I were having none of it. God's call was stronger than ever. Alfred had helped establish several educational institutions by now in India and the South Pacific. God had also given him his heart's desire to see the world. However as is the custom in the east, his missionary parents had dedicated him to full time service in God's house, like Samuel's parents did. But like Jonah, Alfred was trying to run away from God's purpose for Him. Nevertheless, he always felt haunted reading Psalm 139, "Where can I flee from your presence . . . !" and also by the words in the poem, "The Hound of Heaven," which he had read in school years ago. He realized there was no escape from His presence, no matter where in the world he went. And now when the Lord was making possible the impossible, and holding the door open, he had to respond positively. We had to be faithful to our God who is faithful, so very faithful to us.

Thus having brushed the devil aside, we decided to move towards Delhi, the capital city of India, where all the passport offices and embassies are situated and where such matters moved smoothly and quickly, as compared to other towns. The best way to do this would be to find a job, and I began to scan the newspapers for advertisements. Soon I saw one which wanted a lady principal. It was in Lucknow, the capital city of U. P. state, named after Annie Besant, the founder of Theosophy. It was a co-educational college, which was from first grade to twelfth grade, with nearly three thousand students, and a staff of nearly seventy men and women. I was nervous and said I'd never qualify for that post. There'll be many others, far better and experienced educationists who'd apply. No, I wasn't even going to apply. I'd make a complete fool of myself. But then Alfred's faith in God is admirably unshakeable. His adventurous spirit is positive and undaunting. He stops at nothing, and he encouraged me to go ahead and apply. "If God wants it, that job is yours. You do your part and let God do His. Send in your application with a prayer, as more things are wrought by prayer, than this world can dream of, as wrote the great poet Alfred Lord Tennyson in his Morte' de Arthur."

I had my teacher's training and the basic qualifications and experience required, so though hesitatingly, I went ahead and applied, at Alfred's loving encouragement. He desired deeply to promote me to go higher and higher intellectually, culturally and above all spiritually, because I'd come from a very different background.

Imagine my surprise when I was told that my application was accepted, and I was short listed and called for an interview. When I saw the other candidates my heart sank. I had no chance before those mature and apparently more experienced heavy weights, who talked so well. Some of them looked as old as my mother.

At the interview I just answered the questions casually, feeling quite sure I couldn't handle an institution of such magnitude and reputation. Some of the teachers were reaching retirement age, elderly men, I suppose with daughters my age. They'd surely make rings around me, if I was appointed as Principal over them. The very thought gave me cold feet.

After the interview we did window shopping at the town's mall called Hazrat Ganj, had lunch at a restaurant called Kwality and drove back.

Though God lives in eternity, He knows we mortals don't. Two days later I received an urgent phone call from the college manager, informing me that my interview was successful and the Board unanimously decided to offer me the position, and would appreciate it if I accept the offer and take charge immediately. They mentioned the pay scale, which was fabulous, and a few salient features of the terms and conditions involved.

I was absolutely flabbergasted, just couldn't believe it, and was lost for words but gave my reply. Alfred was elated though speechless also. We went down on our knees, thanking God profoundly. Once again God had performed a miracle of wonder. Once again he confirmed our faith. Once again he was saying that if people turn to Him, humble themselves, and pray . . . then will He hear their prayer, and fulfill the desires of their heart. All I could say was—"My Lord, and my God, how great Thou art."

This experience made my soul sing with joy, hope and blessed assurance, and it strengthened my faith further. I began to feel that I could handle the college through Christ who strengthens us. Furthermore, God had granted me Alfred as a gift, to be by my side constantly with global experience in Educational Administration, and so much more. Alfred reminded me of Deuteronomy 31:6, "Be strong, and of good courage, nor be afraid: for the Lord, thy God, He it is that doth go with thee; He will not fail thee, nor forsake thee," and still assured me more with, "As thy days, so shall thy strength be." And also just as Jesus spoke to St. Paul, so did He to me saying, "My grace is sufficient for thee, for my strength is made perfect in weakness." (2 Cor. 12:9).

God had shut a window but opened a door, as an opportunity for me to go a step further on my journey to teach and spread the Word in a larger institution, and larger town. I was once again walking by faith with my hand in His hand and was sure where He guides, He certainly provided, (Psalm 48:14 and Phil. 4:19).

It was time for us to make necessary plans for the care of our school, which I did give to my Vice Principal, and pack my bags, as I was asked to assume my responsibilities immediately. Having done that, we moved on with a new song in our heart to Lucknow, where I took the reigns of Annie Besant College, as Principal.

Two successful years passed by at Annie Besant. I had brought the institution, to the brink of a degree college and ready to open B.A. classes. I had not realized that the Manager who was a staunch Hindu and was opposed to appointing a Christian Principal, was so taken up by my dedicated services as a Christian, that before I left Lucknow he said to me, "I was against having a Christian Principal but seeing your work I have changed my mind and intend to appoint Christian Principals in the future." I praise God that here He had used me as a witness to glorify His name.

Meanwhile we heard from Bethany Theological Seminary at Richmond, Indiana, that they had approved our applications for admission in their M.Div. program. We were thrilled. Alfred remained calm and radiated that strength and assurance that emits from deep and firm faith in our Lord. His non-chalant demeanor was quite eloquent. He was so well grounded in the Scriptures and sacred music, which he personified in his daily walk. It was so comforting and so exhilarating.

However, we still had to obtain our visas and buy air tickets etc. Now we had to move to Delhi to expedite visa and travel facilities. We scanned the newspaper as before, and found an organization which needed a lady principal, experienced in establishing educational institutions. I applied and by His grace was offered the position on temporary basis, which suited us.

Visa and flight arrangements made, we informed Bethany Theological Seminary of our arrival at Dayton Airport on August 21, 2003. We were picked up by a student, and brought to our quarters at about 9.00 p.m. that night. Next morning one of the staff of Bethany Theological Seminary paid us a visit. She informed us that our sponsor suddenly refused to abide by her financial commitment. We thought we'd finally arrived to begin our studies for full time ministry. Now we faced this most unexpected turn of events.

We were literally stunned; we asked her, "What do we do? What happens now? Would we have to go back?" She said she didn't know. The devil was at work again.

Words failed us to express the hollow feelings that surged through us. Here we were in a strange land, full of joy and hope, having made it by the grace of God. As usual Alfred remained calm and said, "America is a big country with a big heart, God will see us through this crisis too. He has called us here to fulfill His plan. Just wait upon the Lord as before. Jesus never fails."

Later in the evening a member of the staff came over and asked us to see the President of the Seminary.

We went to his office and the President told us that they'd do something about our situation. "The Seminary has never faced such a problem before. We are all thrown in a state of utter bewilderment," he said. The President then assured us, "We can never let you go back, we can't do that!" So here we were again, waiting upon our Lord.

Later we were informed that all the staff members of the Seminary had decided to pool in and raise funds for us, while we fill out forms and applications for scholarships etc.

We breathed a deep sigh of relief. We were so grateful to God, the President and to all the staff of Bethany Theological Seminary, who made it possible for us to go forward with the studies and preparation for the ministry. Something they'd never done before. God bless their generous hearts.

Today, having completed my M.Div., I am now the Pastor of the Church of the Brethren at Panora, Iowa. I recall when I wanted to be a nun. But God called me for a wider ministry.

Alfred and I are happy serving the loving congregation of believers. We enjoy serving as a team. They say, "A joy shared is doubled." Theologically Alfred gives me a clearer insight in the Scriptures, and brings out some details in his funny way. As a musician he supports my ministry whole heartedly, by solos, or as song leader, or by playing the piano or organ as the need arises.

Whenever introducing me as pastor, he adds, "And I play the second fiddle." Amazing for an Indian man to admit playing the second fiddle, as humorously, and publicly too, as he does! It is Christ who transforms us. Yes, it is fun to be a Christian, and serving the Lord, with a funny partner, and that's what makes my being a Christian "funnier" everyday.

Today as I look back and write this, I'm reminded of the words of St. Paul, in Romans 8:31-34 "If God be for us, who can be against us who will bring any charge against God's elect."

I have been through the valley of the shadow of death for several years. My journey from Krishna to Christ was fraught with dangers and threats but I have witnessed His mighty hand of salvation. He keeps His Word, every syllable of it, to the very end. It also brings to mind the words of the hymn—

"Standing on the Promises of Christ my King, I cannot fall."

This journey of faith in the saving grace of Christ is a personal experience of those who walk and talk with God daily, and I can testify that it's all the more reason to trust and obey Him. It cannot be explained, it cannot be proved by words, because we are growing daily with the Living Word, who became God's Lamb of flesh and blood to be crucified for us; and rose victorious over sin and death; and it is a mystery how He surrounds us, dwells among us, within us, and we in Him through faith.

In conclusion I'd like to express my deepest gratitude to God, who considered me worthy to be called to serve Him, to Bethany Theological Seminary, who equipped me to study to be approved to serve before man and God, to the Search Committee, congregation, and the Board of Panora Church of the Brethren, to the District Executive of Northern Plains District, Tim Button-Harrison (who is equivalent to the Bishop), and especially to my beloved husband, who not only brought me to Christ, but most lovingly nurtured me in my faith and understanding of the Holy Scriptures, walking hand in hand to fulfill my dreams.

Praise be unto God who gives us the victory!